635.9 Kessell, Mervyn S.
KES
    Rhododendrons and
    azaleas

17.50   85-400

DATE		
JUL 27 1993	JUL 08 1996	
MAR 12 1994	OCT 03 1996	
APR 05 1994	NOV 04 1996	
	JUN 02 1998	
DEC 01 1994	MAR 1 2000	
FEB 09 1995	AUG 08 2000	
JUN 22 1995	JAN 27 2001	
FEB 12 1996		
APR 26 1996		

ink back
pg. 2| 3/03

Rhododendrons and Azaleas

Rhododendrons and Azaleas

Mervyn S. Kessell

85-400

BLANDFORD PRESS

Poole   Dorset

First published in the U.K. 1981 by
Blandford Press
Link House, West Street, Poole, Dorset,
BH15 1LL

Copyright © 1981 Blandford Books Ltd

British Library Cataloguing in Publication Data

Kessell, Mervyn S.
    Rhododendrons and azaleas.
    1. Azalea   2. Rhododendron
    I. Title
    635.9'3362   SB413.R4

ISBN 0 7137 1076 4

Printed and bound in Great Britain by
Morrison & Gibb Ltd, London and
Edinburgh

Contents

Acknowledgements

I would like to thank the following individuals and organisations for their help in producing this book:

Mr J. Basford, Sir Ilay Campbell Bt, Mr D. C. Carmichael, Dr Chamberlain, Dr J. Cullen, Mr M. College, Miss L. Dick, Mr I. Dougall, Dr G. Foster, Mr A. Hall, Mr R. Henfrey (drawings), Mr A. Horgan, Mr I. Jenkins, Mr A. Kenneth, Dr A. Leslie, Dr F. S. MacKenna, Mr A. Maloy, Mr A. Martin, Miss E. Pollock (typing), Mr E. W. Reuthe, Mr M. Woodcock, Mr E. Wright, Mr H. Wright and Dr J. S. Yeates; Kinsealy Research Station, National Gardens Scheme, National Trust, National Trust for Scotland, Royal Botanic Gardens — Edinburgh, Royal Horticultural Society, Scotland Garden Scheme, Scottish Rock Garden Club, West of Scotland Agricultural College, the specialist groups and societies listed in Appendix 6;

and also the following nurseries:

Hilliers, Notcutts, Reuthe, Slococks and Waterers.

Conversion Table

Length	Area	Capacity
1 mm = 0.0394 in	1 cm^2 = 0.155 in^2	1 ml = 0.035 fl oz
1 cm = 0.3937 in	1 m^2 = 1.196 yd^2	1 l = 1.76 pt
1 m = 39.37 in		

Weight	Volume	Temperature
1 gm = 0.0352 oz	1 cm^3 = 0.06102 in^3	$°C \times \frac{9}{5} + 32 = °F$
1 kg = 2.205 lb	1 m^3 = 1.308 yd^3	
1 tonne = 0.984 ton		

Foreword

I first met Mervyn Kessell at a gathering at Findlaystone, home of our doyenne of west coast gardeners, Lady Macmillan of Macmillan, and it was obvious then that he had been fatally bitten by the 'rhododendron bug'. This is not, I hasten to say, *Stephanitis rhododendri*, referred to in the text, but that even more menacing predator which attacks the grower rather than the plant. As yet there is no effective method of control! Shortly thereafter, Mr Kessell moved to Argyll (one of the recognised symptoms of his disorder) and the next of our many subsequent meetings took place at my home.

Lovingly leafing through my volumes of *MILLAIS*, he let fall that he was writing a book on rhododendrons. Inwardly, and I trust silently, I groaned, for behind me, as I sat, were ranged shelves packed with volumes on the subject, and I doubted whether there was room for another. I am now totally convinced there was.

Here is a manual-come-reference book for amateur and commercial grower alike, assembling with admirable clarity an amazing amount of easily digestible facts about rhododendrons, valuable advice on their culture, and much useful, and not always easily available, information as to specialist societies, gardens open to the public and nurseries. The sections on propagation, pests and diseases, and plant associations will, I feel sure, prove of particular interest.

It is unfortunate for the author that his book should appear at a time when feelings run high about the proposed substitution of the Cullen/Chamberlain system of classification for the familiar Balfourian one. The change, which is probably inevitable, will lead to much confusion among gardeners and nurserymen for some time to come, but Mr Kessel has dealt with the subject in a calm and detached manner, and has so arranged his book that it will be able to be used by those familiar with both old and new systems. I heartily commend *Rhododendrons and Azaleas* to all of us who grow and love that most varied and enchanting of genera.

Sir Ilay M. Campbell

Preface

The full beauty of the vast range of plants now grown under the generic name *Rhododendron* only becomes apparent as the gardener begins to discover new species.

Despite the fact that many species have been in cultivation for well over a hundred years, comparatively few enthusiastic gardeners have ever grown more than two or three types. Perhaps the mystique surrounding their nomenclature, and the mistaken belief that very few are hardy enough to be grown out of doors, has contributed to this. It is unfortunately true that the names of some of the species can be rather offputting until examined in detail and it is then that the non-Latin scholars begin to realise just why such weird and wonderful names have been applied to this beautiful group of plants.

Although most species and hybrids flourish to great effect in the temperate zones throughout the world, there are many other less favourable climates in which a few species at least can be persuaded to grow, given the correct treatment by the horticulturist.

This book has therefore been written as a beginners' guide to the mysterious world of the *Rhododendron* and is not meant, in any way, to be a definitive work. I have tried, where possible, to simplify the botanical side of the cultivation but this has not always been possible. I have deliberately included a reasonably comprehensive list of books, for the key to greater knowledge is knowing where to find the relevant information. For example, despite the new classification, which undoubtedly will be accepted for the most part by the botanical world, the Royal Horticultural Society's *Rhododendron Handbook 1980* (dealing with species) will remain very useful as a means of identification for many years to come. The new generation of rhododendron-growers will probably learn only the new names but the older enthusiast might have a harder time trying to work with both systems — only time will tell.

The many specialist societies and botanical gardens (included are National Trust and many fine private gardens) are the best places to seek a greater insight into this fascinating genus.

Like any other subject, the more one learns, the more one realises that the learning process has only just begun and that even the professional rhododendron-growers seldom claim to know it all. It is also exciting to think that there may be species still undiscovered in the Himalayas.

Any bias which I have towards species of *Rhododendron*, as opposed to hybrids, is because there is a relatively finite number and I could conceivably become familiar with the majority in cultivation. Not all species are necessarily attractive, but many are interesting and tend to become collector's items. However, I could not even attempt to see, let alone learn, the names and values of the thousands of hybrids which have been raised in the last 50 years. On the other hand, hybrids must have some merit or they will not become commercially successful. Many are bred for a specific purpose and tend to be more hardy than many of the species while retaining the flowering characteristics of their more tender parents.

Certain plant-groups, such as the orchids, cacti and succulents, because they are largely greenhouse species, at least in cooler climates, tend to be grown as a monoculture. The *Rhododendron* should not be grown in this fashion as other plants are required to complement and contrast with their beauty. With this in mind, I have included lists of plants which associate well with rhododendrons.

The colour illustrations will, I hope, make an important contribution, for I feel that even the best description does not conjure up the majesty of form and colour to be found in rhododendrons.

Enthusiasm is the key to horticulture and, despite the occasional failures, the rewards are great.

Mervyn Kessell

To my wife Helen and son Stephen
for their tolerance during the writing of this book

History of the Genus

The Rhododendron in Relation to the Plant Kingdom

If one examines the plant kingdom as a whole, an individual species will be seen as only a very small part of a vast range of seed-bearing plants which amount to about 120,000 species.

Although this book is designed to be horticultural rather than botanical in nature, it is useful to understand the relationship of the rhododendron to its allies in the plant world. For this reason the following family tree has been included.

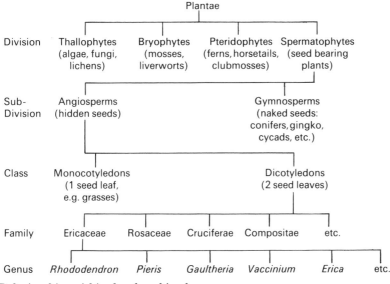

Relationships within the plant kingdom.

Rhododendron is probably the largest of all the genera of woody plants, containing in the region of 770 species, although this does not take into account subspecies and naturally occurring varieties. There are about 300 species in the section VIREYA, although it is almost certain that there are many more still to be discovered, and 162 in the sections RHODODENDRON and POGONANTHUM. *Hymenanthes* has about 210

11

species while the remaining 6 subgenera of the Azalea group contain a total of about 100 species.

Revision of the Classification of the Genus

An assemblage of material concerning the history and methods of *Rhododendron* classification is contained in the publication *Contributions Towards a Classification of Rhododendrons* (Luteyn and O'Brien, 1980). This book contains the papers presented by the world's leading authorities on the present revision of the genus and deals in great detail with virtually every aspect and reason for the change from the series classification of Bayley Balfour. Although it is a complicated and very deep publication for the beginner it is well worth obtaining a copy for future reference.

In simple terms the revision divides the genus into 8 subgenera.

The largest subgenus, *Rhododendron*, has been divided into 3 sections all of which possess leaf scales:

(a) VIREYA, which contains principally the Malesian species, was revised by Sleumer in 1966. The Malesian species form a group of tropical plants which are normally too tender to be grown outdoors in temperate climates and many look quite unlike the species with which we are usually familiar.

(b) RHODODENDRON, which contains 27 subsections, comprising the majority of lepidote or scaly species which we commonly find in temperate gardens and corresponding very approximately (but there have been some significant changes) to the similar sounding names of the old Balfourian system. It can be seen from the list below that all subsection names end with the letter 'a'. This is perhaps the easiest way to distinguish which classification is being used in a text. (In the series list, the majority of names end with the letters 'um', 'e', or 'i'.)

(c) POGONANTHUM comprises 13 species of which none reach a height of more than 1 m and the majority are no more than 30 cm high.

The subgenus *Hymenanthes* contains one section, PONTICUM, and 24 subsections. These contain all the familiar larger-growing non-scaly (elepidote) shrubs, except those of the Azalea group. As with RHODODENDRON above, all subsection names end with the letter 'a'.

The old Azalea group, which is still under revision by the Philipsons in New Zealand at the time of writing, is expected to contain 6 subgenera and 9 sections. However, the actual number of species has yet to be fixed.

Genus: *Rhododendron*

Subgenus: *Rhododendron*
  Section: VIREYA
    Subsection: Pseudovireya, Siphonovireya, Phaeovireya, Albovireya, Solenovireya, Euvireya
  Section: RHODODENDRON
    Subsection: Edgeworthia, Maddenia, Moupinensia, Monantha, Triflora, Scabrifolia, Heliolepida, Carolinia, Lapponica, Rhododendron, Rhododrastra, Saluenensia, Fragarifolia, Uniflora, Cinnabarina, Tephropepla, Virgata, Micrantha, Boothia, Camelliflora, Glauca, Campylogyna, Genestieriana, Lepidota, Baileya, Trichoclada, Afghanica
  Section: POGONANTHUM

Subgenus: *Hymenanthes*
  Section: PONTICUM
    Subsection: Arborea, Argyrophylla, Auriculata, Barbata, Campylocarpa, Campanulata, Falconera, Fortunea, Fulva, Glischra, Grandia, Irrorata, Maculifera, Neriiflora, Parishia, Selensia, Taliensia, Ponticum, Thomsonia, Williamsiana, Fulgensia, Griersoniana, Lanata, Venatora

Subgenus: *Pentanthera*
  Section: PENTANTHERA
       RHODORA
       SCIADORHODON
       VISCIDIFOLIA

Subgenus: *Tsutsutsi*
  Section: BRACHYCALYX
       TASHIROI
       TSUTSUTSI

Subgenus: Azaleastrum
  Section: AZALEASTRUM
       CHIONASTRUM

Subgenus: *Candidastrum*

Subgenus: *Mumeazalea*

Subgenus: *Therorodion*

Revision of the genus Rhododendron *by Sleumer (section VIREYA), Cullen (1980), Chamberlain (1981) and W. R. and M. N. Philipson (Azalea group—under revision).*

Using the old classification, which was designed as a temporary measure by Sir Isaac Bayley Balfour of the Royal Botanic Gardens, Edinburgh, as a basis, between about 1916 and 1925, the species were assembled and published in 1930 by the Royal Horticultural Society under the title *The Species of Rhododendron* (edited by J. B. Stevenson). The system was not intended as a final solution to the classification of the genus but merely as a stop-gap measure during a period when there was a great influx of new material from the field.

The following list is based on the Series Classification adopted in the *Rhododendron Handbook 1980 — Rhododendron Species in Cultivation*, published by the Royal Horticultural Society. The Royal Horticultural Society have also proposed another classification, based on that of Cullen and Chamberlain (1980 and probably 1981), which is designed to be a compromise solution for the horticulturist who wishes to be able to identify distinct clones.

Evolution

Certain authorities believe that the evolution of the rhododendron began 50 million years ago and that the genus is still evolving today, but, because of the vast time scale involved, these changes are almost imperceptible. These authorities consider that the large-leaved species are the most primitive as they show fewer adaptations to their environment than, for instance, the small-leaved *R. lapponicum* from the Arctic, but there is little concrete evidence to prove this.

Distribution

The uninitiated may well be forgiven for thinking that one species, *R. ponticum*, is native to the British Isles, for it grows so well there, especially in the west of Scotland, that it now, in common with *R. luteum*, has gained a place for itself in the *Flora of the British Isles* (Clapham, Tutin and Warburg, 1952).

There are only 6 species native to Europe: *RR. ferrugineum* and *hirsutum* found in the Alps, *R. myrtifolium* in Bulgaria and Yugoslavia, *R. ponticum* in Spain, Portugal and Greece, *R. luteum* in Poland and Eastern Europe and *R. lapponicum* in Arctic regions.

The collector in North America will find about 27 species among his native flora, while, in Australia, *R. lochae* is the only representative.

In the Far East, the total number of species amounts to about 31,

Series	Subseries	Series	Subseries
1 Albiflorum		24 Irroratum	Irroratum
2 Anthopogon			Parishii
3 Arboreum	Arboreum	25 Lacteum	
	Argyrophyllum	26 Lapponicum	
4 Auriculatum		27 Lepidotum	Baileyi
	Canadense		Lepidotum
	Luteum	28 Maddenii	Ciliicalyx
5 Azalea	Nipponicum		Maddenii
	Obtusum		Megacalyx
	Schlippenbachii	29 Micranthum	
	Barbatum	30 Moupinense	
6 Barbatum	Crinigerum		Forrestii
	Glischrum	31 Neriiflorum	Haematodes
	Maculiferum		Neriiflorum
	Boothii		Sanguineum
7 Boothii	Megeratum	32 Ovatum	
	Tephropeplum	33 Ponticum	Caucasicum
8 Camelliiflorum			Ponticum
9 Campanulatum		34 Saluenense	
10 Campylogynum		35 Scabrifolium	
11 Camtschaticum		36 Semibarbatum	
12 Carolinianum		37 Stamineum	
13 Cinnabarinum			Adenogynum
14 Dauricum		38 Taliense	Roxieanum
15 Edgeworthii			Taliense
16 Falconeri			Wasonii
17 Ferrugineum			Campylocarpum
	Calophytum		Cerasinum
	Davidii	39 Thomsonii	Selense
18 Fortunei	Fortunei		Souliei
	Griffithianum		Thomsonii
	Orbiculare		Williamsianum
	Oreodoxa	40 Trichocladum	
19 Fulvum			Augustinii
20 Glaucophyllum	Genestieranum	41 Triflorum	Hanceanum
	Glaucophyllum		Triflorum
21 Grande			Yunnanense
22 Griersonianum		42 Uniflorum	
23 Heliolepis		43 Virgatum	

Rhododendron Series Classification.

including the now very popular *R. yakushimanum* of the Pontica subsection and many members of the old Azalea series (now split into new groupings). New Guinea and Malaysia provide well over 200 species while the remaining 400 or so inhabit the most famous regions of all for rhododendrons, the Sino-Himalayan mountains, western China, Tibet, Burma, Nepal, north India and Afghanistan.

Introduction of the Species

Since horticulture was very much in the ascendancy during the early part of the seventeenth century, it was inevitable that the wealthy landowners and merchants who had a keen interest in gardening, would desire to improve their collections by acquiring new species.

Although the British merchant navy ventured to nearly all parts of the known world, very few plants, other than potential food crops, were ever seriously collected until early in the last century. The task of introducing ornamental plants therefore fell to the specialist collector, such as the naturalist and traveller, John Tradescant Senior.

There appears to be some confusion over the actual date of introduction of the first species of *Rhododendron* to the British Isles, but 1656 is regarded as the year when John Tradescant Junior catalogued the plants in his family garden and listed *R. hirsutum* amongst them.

With the expansion of the British colonies in North America, during the early part of the eighteenth century, horticulture flourished and a flood of hardy imports, including rhododendrons, was soon reaching Europe. Surprisingly, it was not until about 1763 (there is doubt as to the exact date) that *R. ponticum* was first introduced from southern Spain and cultivated in British gardens. The late eighteenth century saw the introduction of several species from North America while, in 1780, Anthony Chaumier found *R. dauricum* in Siberia. *R. luteum (Azalea pontica)* was discovered in 1700 near the Black Sea but, as with other species found in similar circumstances, the actual introduction to horticulture did not take place until much later and, in the case of this particular example, not till 1793.

More species were introduced over the following few years until the beginning of the nineteenth century, when the expansion of western influence in Asia bore fruit for the rest of the horticultural world. From India, in the first decade of the nineteenth century, came *R. arboreum* which, over the last 180 years has been used widely in the production of many magnificent hybrids, not all, unfortunately, completely hardy. In about 1808, *R. simsii* (then known as *Azalea indica*), a shrub used extensively as a parent of the well-known greenhouse hybrids, was introduced. The nomenclature of this particular species has caused considerable confusion over the past 100 years, especially to those enthusiasts who are trying to separate it from the plant known as *R. indicum*.

Another important introduction from the United States of America at about this time was *R. catawbiense* which, when crossed with *R. ponticum* and other species, gave rise to a race of rhododendron known as the Hardy Hybrids. Although the great influx of Himalayan rhododendrons had not yet begun, *R. campanulatum* was introduced from Nepal in 1825. Within what was then the British Empire were countries such as Canada and Ceylon (now Sri Lanka), from whence came, respectively, *R. lapponicum* in 1825 and *R. zeylanicum* (this species is now known as *R. arboreum* subsp. *zeylanicum*). *R. thomsonii*, discovered by Hooker in 1849, flowered in Britain about 8 years later.

In 1895, *R. wardii* was discovered by the Reverend J. A. Soulie but named *R. mussotii*, although it was never officially published under this name. Later, however, Kingdon-Ward, during his 1913 expedition, found the plant in the North Yunnan and it was this re-introduction that was later named by W. W. Smith as *R. wardii* in 1914. Fortunately these two species, *RR. thomsonii* and *wardii* have proved useful as parents, and many fine hybrids such as 'Cornish Cross' (*griffithianum* x *thomsonii*) and 'Crest' (Lady Bessborough x *wardii*) have resulted.

Collection of Rhododendrons

Many people have contributed to the study of rhododendrons by work on classification, physiology and cultivation, sponsorship of plantings and expeditions and by collecting in the field. Tribute must be paid to those no longer alive, such as Sir William Wright Smith, Mr E. H. M. Cox and the Reverend Crutwell.

Expeditions are still continuing today, sponsored by such bodies as the Royal Horticultural Society, the Botanic Gardens of Edinburgh and Kew, and by private individuals. Accounts of these expeditions, by Peter Cox, A. D. Schilling, Jeremy and Sayers and others, can be found in the Royal Horticultural Society publications. At least one interesting fact emerges from the history of plant collecting, and that is the part played by politics in obtaining access to a country. Western China was at one time open to collectors, then the borders were closed. Now, hopefully, the rich flora may one day again be visited by the western traveller if the relaxation in government restrictions continues.

MAJOR COLLECTORS

Reginald Farrer, 1880–1920 Reginald Farrer was born in Yorkshire in 1880 and spent much of his life travelling and writing books about his expeditions to various parts of the world. Two of his expeditions, the first to Kansu in 1914–1915, and the second to Upper Burma in 1919, produced some interesting species, although many had been recorded by earlier collectors.

George Forrest, 1873–1932   George Forrest was possibly the most prolific collector the horticultural world has ever known. At the beginning of the twentieth century, following in the footsteps of many other famous Scots, Forrest travelled abroad to seek his fortune, visiting Australia and South Africa. On his return to Scotland in 1902, in the hope of obtaining an interesting position, he applied to the Royal Botanic Gardens in Edinburgh. Fortunately he was offered a post in the herbarium, where he continued working for 2 years until 1904, when Mr A. K. Bulley of Cheshire contacted the Gardens seeking someone to carry out explorations for him in western China.

Forrest's first expedition to the Tali and Mekong areas almost ended in disaster, when he was attacked by natives, who were, at that time, constantly fighting to avoid invasion of their territory.

In 1910 he continued to explore the valleys from Burma to the Yunnan, paying particular attention to Teng-yueh, the Shweli-Salween divide and the Tali-lichiang mountain ranges.

His third expedition, which was financed by J. C. Williams of Caerhays Castle, lasted from 1912–1915 and covered a similarly difficult area, but in this case fraught with dangers due to rebel armies.

Organisational ability was a talent which George Forrest certainly did not lack, as has been shown from the magnitude of his collections. He trained natives to carry out much of the exploratory work which he could not possibly have managed on his own. The collection and drying of plant materials was almost on a factory scale, with 35 presses being operated at one time. Forrest reported in letters to J. C. Williams, that he also had cleaned and dried over 45 kg of seed. The potential number of plants which could be germinated from this quantity of seed is phenomenal, even allowing for fairly high losses due to poor storage conditions.

Further expeditions were embarked on by Forrest in 1917–1919, 1921–1922, 1924–1925 and 1930–1931. On 6 January 1932, he collapsed and died near Teng-yueh, where he was buried.

For the connoisseur wishing to learn of the vast range of rhododendrons which Forrest collected, the *Rhododendron Handbook 1980* on species is essential reading.

Robert Fortune, 1812–1880   Robert Fortune, who was born in the Scottish border county of Berwickshire, worked for a period, like many other famous Scottish collectors, in the Royal Botanic Gardens, Edinburgh. He was employed by the Royal Horticultural Society to collect plants from the Far East. The bulk of the plants which he brought back were collected within a few miles of the eastern coast of China. He is credited with the introduction of several forms of *R. obtusum*.

Sir J. D. Hooker, 1817–1911   In 1847, Sir J. D. Hooker left Britain for India on what was to become an epic voyage. He journeyed northwards to the Sikkim Himalayas and, by 1851, had discovered 45 species, including *Rhododendron thomsonii, campylocarpum, falconeri, grande* and *maddenii*. For the next 50 years, several more species were added to those already in cultivation. Others remained only as herbarium specimens but were often introduced successfully by later collectors.

Frank Kingdon-Ward, 1885–1958   Frank Kingdon-Ward was born in Cambridge in 1885. His interest in plants no doubt derived from his father, who was Professor of Botany at Cambridge University. Next to George Forrest, Kingdon-Ward probably had as much to do with the successful introduction of the genus as any collector in the last hundred years. Practically every garden in the country with collections at least 30 years old contain a few of Kingdon-Ward's original seedlings. It is an interesting hobby to wander around some of the now derelict or declining gardens of the large estates and discover, among the rotting vegetation at the bottom of the large rhododendrons, old labels with Kingdon-Ward numbers, which must refer to original material rather than just layers from the Kingdon-Ward stock.

Kingdon-Ward's first expedition took place in 1909–1910, when, with another collector, by the name of Malcolm Anderson, he travelled to western China. Sponsorship was, of course, an important feature of any expedition and, fortunately, he was financed by Mr A. K. Bulley, Lord Aberconway, Lionel de Rothschild and many others who were keen to acquire the new plants which were now arriving from the Sino-Himalayas.

While rhododendrons were perhaps the most widely collected genus, beautiful species of *Primula* and *Lilium* were among the many other genera brought back. This is undoubtedly why these species are so often found growing in association with rhododendrons in our gardens today.

The years of the main expeditions to the Sino-Himalayas are as follows: 1913–1914, 1919, 1921, 1922, 1924–1925, 1926, 1927–1928, 1931, 1933, 1935, 1937, 1938–1939, 1946, 1948, 1949, 1950, 1953 and 1956. Details of the rhododendron species collected can be found in the *Rhododendron Handbook 1980*.

As well as being a great collector, Kingdon-Ward wrote many books about his expeditions.

Frank Ludlow, 1886–1972   Frank Ludlow took part in four major expeditions of interest to the rhododendron enthusiast, all of which were to the Sino-Himalayas; these were during the years 1938, 1939–1941, 1942–1945, 1946–1947 and 1949.

Edward Madden, 1805–1856   Edward Madden, Irish by birth, spent much of his early life in India where he served as a Lieutenant-Colonel in the British Army. This period of service allowed him to collect many plants, including several rhododendron species, which later proved extremely valuable.

Dr Joseph F. Rock, 1884–1962   Dr Rock was born in Vienna in 1884 but later moved to the Hawaiian islands where he became Professor of Botany at the College of Hawaii. Several expeditions to Tibet and Yunnan were undertaken under the patronage of the United States Department of Agriculture and the National Geographical Society of Washington. Many interesting and useful species were discovered or introduced during the expeditions of 1923, 1924, 1925, 1926, 1929 and 1932. Large numbers of the original seedlings are still to be found growing in gardens throughout the world.

George Sherriff, 1898–1967   George Sherriff O.B.E., who was born in Stirlingshire, Scotland, in 1892, spent his early career in the British Army and was for some time stationed on the north-west frontier of India. Sherriff undertook several expeditions, mainly with Frank Ludlow and others, to Bhutan and Tibet, in the years 1933, 1934, 1936, 1937, 1938, 1939, 1941, 1943, 1946, 1947 and 1949.

Ernest Henry Wilson, 1876–1930   Ernest Henry Wilson, an Englishman by birth, embarked on the first of two expeditions to western China in 1899 for the British nursery firm of James Veitch and Son. A further two expeditions were made to China under the auspices of the Arnold Arboretum, the last, in 1910, with joint sponsorship from British subscribers. On his journeys, many new *Rhododendron* species were discovered or others re-introduced to cultivation, including the famous 'Wilson's Fifty' Kurume azaleas.

COLLECTOR'S NUMBERS

In order to provide a positive means of identifying the specific area, group of plants or individual plant from which a seed or dried specimen originates, collector's numbers are used. These numbers, which are often seen in botanic gardens or similar establishments, alongside the genus and species, are prefixed by the initials of the collector or collectors who sent or brought them back from the field, e.g. KW 7724 refers to *R*.

macabeanum collected by Kingdon-Ward on his 1927–1928 expedition to Assam and the Mishmi Hills (see *Rhododendron Handbook 1980*). By consulting the field notes, a more precise location can be found if required.

The situation frequently arises where the same species is collected by two or more people in different localities on different expeditions, and this single species may therefore have several collector's numbers. Horticulturists generally hope that, by trying out different collector's numbers, improved hardiness, habit or flower colour may be obtained. The situation can, however, be confused by the seedlings which are distributed under the same collector's number, because open pollination in the wild can lead to a considerable variance in the progeny. If a particularly good form is found, this may be given a clonal name and submitted to the Royal Horticultural Society for an award.

A typical example is *R. vellereum* 'Far Horizon' which was given an Award of Merit on 18 April 1979. The species was collected by Kingdon-Ward under number KW 5656. The clonal name 'Far Horizon' identifies the seedling itself. From then on, identical plants can be produced only by vegetative propagation.

Hybrids

A hybrid can be a cross between two species, two hybrids, a species and a hybrid or, less commonly, two genera. The genus *Rhododendron* can be divided into two groups, the lepidotes, which have scales, and the elepidotes, which lack them. For genetic reasons these two groups are almost impossible to cross and any attempt to produce hybrids between members of these two sections is unlikely to be successful (although one has been achieved). The reasons for hybridisation are similar to those for selection of forms among species: improvement in colour, hardiness, habit, flowering times. In many cases, especially among amateurs, it is purely the fascination of producing a new plant of one's own.

Hybrids are being produced and marketed in ever-increasing numbers. In 1979–1980 alone, about 190 new names were added to the *International Rhododendron Register*; needless to say only a fraction of these will ever become a commercial success. It is a regrettable fact of commercial life that hybrids, or for that matter species which prove difficult to propagate, seldom become available to the general public due to the inevitable high cost of production. This does not necessarily mean, however, that those not found in the nurserymen's catalogues are of little value. Indeed, there are still a few nurseries prepared to grow a selection of the uncommon species and hybrids.

The code of practice which governs the naming of all new hybrids has done much to reduce the confusion which was prevalent prior to the early 1950s. The former practice of giving hybrids a Latin name has thankfully long been discontinued. A typical example of such a plant is *R.* x *praecox* (*ciliatum* x *dauricum*) which was often, and still can be, found in certain places, written as *R. praecox*. Botanical Latin names are now reserved solely for species and naturally occurring varieties found in the wild.

Two other terms, grex and clone, will frequently be encountered in *Rhododendron* nomenclature. Grex is a name derived from the Latin, meaning flock, and is applied to all the progeny of a cross e.g. *R.* x *loderi*.

If an individual plant from among the many seedlings grown under the grex name shows particular merit, it might be given a clonal name, e.g. *R. loderi* 'Sir Joseph Hooker'. The clonal name is always written with single inverted commas in a general text but is frequently omitted in catalogues or where lists of hybrids appear in different publications. The essential fact to remember is that a clone, once named, can be maintained only by vegetative propagation.

HYBRIDISTS

Amongst the nurserymen who raised and distributed many of the original hybrids and species of *Rhododendron,* such names as Cunningham of Edinburgh, Vilmorin of France, Waterer of Knaphill, come to mind.

Today, hardy hybrids are available from most garden centres. However, specialist nurseries, e.g. Cox, Exbury Gardens, Reuthe and Hobbie (Appendix 9) are still raising and distributing new cultivars. Many of the more recent cultivars to win prizes at the show bench have been raised by amateurs, such as Loder, Magor, Stephenson-Clarke and many others in the United States of America, Canada and New Zealand.

Cultivation

Site

SELECTION

There are probably very few private individuals who have a great deal of choice in the matter of a site for planting rhododendrons, unless they have gardens large enough, and with a sufficiently varied vegegation, to provide several micro-climates. Quite often, the garden is next to the house and it may face in the wrong direction, suffer from strong prevailing winds, have an alkaline soil, or other misfortune, any of which can make life difficult for the horticulturist. Usually, however, there are ways around such problems and this section will attempt to demonstrate a few of them.

ASPECT

A few species of *Rhododendron* can be grown in almost any aspect, with the exception of areas immediately adjacent to buildings, which, as a result, receive no sun at any time of the day. In a situation such as this, foliage tends to lack colour and is rather drawn. Consequently, the plants seldom, if ever, produce flowers.

An eastern aspect is in many ways the most difficult to manage. The problems arise in spring, when flower buds start to open while frosts are still prevalent. The sudden rise in temperature as the early morning sun strikes the petals will cause much more damage than if the buds were allowed to thaw out slowly.

SHELTER

The localities in which rhododendrons are to be found growing in the wild are excellent indicators of the conditions which they require in cultivation. The alpine species, such as *RR. ferrugineum* and *hirsutum,* with their small, tough, leathery leaves, grow admirably well in full sun while the large-leaved species require a degree of protection from cold drying winds and strong summer sun.

The woodland garden is ideal for the majority of medium to large species as the trees provide the correct balance of shade and wind protection. A mixture of coniferous and deciduous trees should be selected and planted to give shade in the hottest part of the day. It should be noted, however, that excessive shading can severely hinder flower bud formation. In some of the larger woodland gardens, such as Ben More and Arduaine in Scotland, the removal of very large trees has had the effect of encouraging some of the large-leaved species to flower for the first time in many years.

Wind damage can often cause havoc among the large-leaved species and a specimen of R. *macabeanum*, growing in a garden at Largs, had its entire complement of leaves stripped from it during one winter gale, although, interestingly enough, it recovered completely the following year. It should also be noted that severe turbulence can be experienced when strong winds are reflected off house walls.

In small gardens, it is impossible to plant large trees for shelter and it is therefore advisable to concentrate on those species of *Rhododendron* which are considered extremely hardy under adverse conditions (see Appendix 1). When experience has been gained, the more tender species can be tried, using shelter provided by larger established shrubs or artificial windbreaks.

WINDBREAKS

Windbreaks are invaluable, especially in coastal regions, where damage from salt-laden wind (frequently recorded as much as 32 km inland) can prove fatal to many plants. The effects of winds on plants can be quite dramatic and, once in a while, a hurricane will occur in areas not normally prone to such events, as demonstrated by the great storm of January 1968, in which large parts of central Scotland were totally devastated. So severe were the winds that large old plants of R. *ponticum* were torn out by the roots.

Table 1 shows the types of barrier and the optimum distance from them for planting. It can be seen that the medium dense windbreak is the most effective; the greatest protection occurs at a distance five times its own height and, thereafter, falls off more gradually than in the other types. Windbreaks should be at least twelve times as long as they are high, to prevent wind from cutting around the ends. A list of plants suitable for use as windbreaks is included in Appendix 4.

Table 1   Effect of barriers on wind speed.

Permeability of barrier	Percentage of wind speed in the open at given distances from the barrier (h = height of barrier)							
	0	2h	5h	10h	15h	20h	25h	30h
70%	90	80	70	75	85	90	95	100
50%	40	25	20	25	50	60	75	90
0%	0	20	40	65	80	85	95	100

FROST AND FROST POCKETS

Frost frequency in a garden is determined by general climate, geographical situation, local topography and the design of the garden. The general climate of a country is related to latitude and the limitations that it imposes on the species which can be grown must be accepted. However, geographical situation will have a modifying effect and you may be able to choose whether or not to live by the coast or inland, in the north, south, west or east, or on high or low ground. Temperature, exposure and rainfall will vary accordingly. Local topography can have a very marked effect in regard to frost incidence. Although generally speaking, the frost incidence increases with altitude, local frost pockets will form quite readily at the bottom of a gentle slope when there is no means of escape for cold air. This is because, on a calm clear night, the air near the ground cools, becomes heavier, and tends to slide downhill.

Effect of Garden Design   The design of the garden is one factor over which the grower has some control. Even with a relatively small garden the risk of the formation of one or more frost pockets is quite high but this risk can be reduced.

Flat gardens which lie at the bottom of a slope may suffer from the effects of a cold air dam. In this situation, cold air flows down into the garden from a neighbouring garden and goes no further, simply because of the expanse of flat ground. This can be prevented by constructing a dense hedge or solid wall on the side of the garden from which the cold air flows. The cold air will now have to build up to the level of the wall before it spills over into the garden.

In a garden on a slope, the presence of a wall or dense hedge will almost certainly be the main reason for the formation of a frost pocket. Removal of such an obstruction will most probably solve this problem.

25

Protection from Frost   In commercial fruit orchards, where damage to flowers can lead to financial losses, steps are frequently taken to minimise the occurrence of frosts. The methods used include fans for circulating the air, burning straw bales and, most commonly, overhead spraying with water.

These methods are seldom, if ever, employed by the commercial nurseryman, as the blossoms of the rhododendron are of very little significance, frost damage to the foliage of the larger types is in most cases of minor importance and the smaller species tend to be more hardy. However, certain species, principally of the Maddenii series (Maddenii subsection), are often brought into the greenhouse to flower because of their susceptibility to frost damage.

DRAINAGE

With the exception of marginal waterplants, there are few trees and shrubs which will tolerate waterlogging to any extent, since roots must have a readily available oxygen supply in the soil. Plants will die if deprived of oxygen for any length of time and waterlogged soil is deficient in air spaces. Drainage can be improved by the addition of tile drains, but this is seldom carried out unless the conditions are so bad that severe ponding is taking place.

The majority of gardens are built on slopes where natural drainage is usually sufficient to prevent waterlogging. The construction of raised beds will often improve drainage and improving the structure of a heavy clay soil is frequently all that is necessary. Specimen plants are often grown on a mound when drainage is a problem, but these mounds must be large enough both to discourage the roots from growing down towards the stagnant water in search of nourishment and to prevent them from being scorched on the surface.

Soil

Soil is the result of the weathering of underlying rock or of deposition by rivers or glaciers. There are over a million different types of soil in the world and, within one garden, there can be considerable variation. Soil is made up of coarse and fine sands, silts and clays, soluble mineral salts, humus, water and air and its properties are related to the proportions in which these constituents occur.

TEXTURE

The texture of a soil is determined primarily by particle size (Table 2).

Table 2 Soil constituents and particle size.

Soil constituent	Particle size in mm diameter
Coarse sand	0.2–2
Fine sand	0.02–0.2
Silt	0.0002–0.02
Clay	Below 0.002

The percentage of each constituent determines the type of soil, e.g. a sandy soil is one containing over 70% sand whereas a clay soil usually contains over 40% clay particles. Loam is intermediate between the two. The texture of the soil can be changed by the addition of clay or sand, but this may not in itself materially alter the structure.

STRUCTURE

Structure is concerned with the arrangement of the soil particles. In sandy soils, the particles tend to function independently whereas, in clay soils, different-sized particles are bound together by colloidal materials. Structure can be most easily determined by crushing a lump of soil between the fingers. If the particles do not stick together, the structure is poor. This is usually a feature of sandy soils lacking in organic material. On the other hand, if, despite considerable pressure, the soil only compresses and does not break up, this also indicates a poor structure, but one normally associated with heavy clays. The ideal soil structure is found in the loams which break up under gentle pressure.

Rhododendrons, like most plants, require an ample supply of water but their roots must on no account become waterlogged. The correct soil structure is therefore vitally important as it affects the passage of water through the soil and the air content of the soil.

In a very heavy soil with a high clay content, the spaces surrounding each particle, if they exist at all, are very small and drainage and aeration are poor. A sandy soil with large particles, although well aerated, will allow water to percolate through it but, during dry conditions, will not retain sufficient water to encourage root development. This will result in flagging foliage and poor flower quality. There is also a danger of nutrients being leached away.

IMPROVEMENT OF POOR STRUCTURE

The addition of sand or grit, and the action of winter frosts, will improve heavy clay soils, and organic matter of a coarse strawy nature will also help the process. Lime is often used on acid clays to improve the structure but it should never be used on soils where it is intended to grow rhododendrons or other Ericaceae.

Organic matter is one of the best weapons at the horticulturalist's disposal. This material is broken down by soil organisms into a black colloidal substance, known as humus, which has the capacity to coat each individual soil particle. This coating cements together the particles until a 'crumb' is built up. There are a variety of organic materials which can be used to improve soil structure.

Peat   There are two types of peat used in horticulture, sphagnum and sedge, although the former is more commonly employed as a soil conditioner. Certain fen peats must be avoided as their pH level is too high for the successful cultivation of rhododendrons. The coarser grades are quite satisfactory and, in certain cases, even preferable.

Peat can be incorporated into the soil at any time of the year by digging, forking or, on a larger scale, rotavating; the best mix will be achieved during drier weather. The proportion of peat to soil is difficult to quantify because of the variability in soil types, but a ratio of 1:1 is not thought to be too high. Under normal conditions, peat becomes totally assimilated into the soil within 1 or 2 years.

Crushed Tree Bark   Tree bark is a waste product of sawmills and for many years was not seen to have any particular use. Recently, however, crushed or pulverised tree bark has come to replace or supplement peat in some localities due to its lower cost and ready availability. It is generally obtainable in various degrees of decomposition, which depend on the length of time it has been stacked after the crushing operation. The size of particles can be controlled by passing the bark through screens of different mesh sizes.

Crushed bark can be bought in bags at garden centres or, frequently, in bulk from a distributor. The principal advantage which bark has over peat is the longer period which it takes to decompose. This varies according to the extent to which it has been pulverised.

Tree bark should not be used immediately after the crushing process as it has been reported that resins detrimental to plants are released. In practice, I have been using crushed tree bark for many years with no adverse effects, although the material has always been stacked for 2 to 3 months prior to use. Tree bark purchased in bags will have been thoroughly processed before being put on sale to the public.

Although of little nutrient value, analysis has given the following results for coarsely pulverised bark: nitrogen 0.30% (5 p.p.m. as a nitrate), phosphorus 6 p.p.m., potassium 155 p.p.m., magnesium 36 p.p.m.

Leafmould   Leafmould is an excellent soil conditioning agent for use in rhododendron cultivation, providing that it has not been collected in an area of alkaline soil. The best leafmould comes from beech and oak and, in many cases, the presence of tannic acid in the latter may be an added advantage. However, as long as the leafmould is well rotted, almost any type will suffice (providing there is no obvious disease present).

Conifer Needles   Conifer needles, especially spruce, are ideally suited for use in composts and as soil conditioners. A recent report has stated that the needles contain a poisonous resin and should be avoided. This may perhaps be true in the vegetable garden but as far as acid-loving plants are concerned, I am convinced that conifer needles help to promote an extremely prolific root system.

Before gathering any needles on private land, be sure to get permission. Conifer needles should be avoided if there is any indication that honey fungus (*Armillaria mellea*) is present.

Sawdust   Where supplies are available, sawdust is worth considering as a soil conditioner, providing the following points are taken into account. As with several other actively decaying organic materials, sawdust is broken down by various nitrifying bacteria which initially extract nitrogen from the surrounding soil. This can lead to a temporary nitrogen deficiency and so a supplementary feed of ammonium sulphate should be given, at a rate of 56 g/m². The rate of application is difficult to determine as it varies with the state of decay of the sawdust.

Animal Manures   Animal manures from horses or cows can be used as soil conditioners provided that they are well rotted. These manures are particularly good where large quantities of straw have been incorporated in the bedding. Slurry, however, should not be used as, quite apart from the foul smell, there appears to be some evidence in agricultural circles that it has a deleterious effect on the soil structure.

SOIL pH

Strictly speaking the pH of a substance is a measure of its hydrogen ion concentration. More simply, it is a measure of acidity/alkalinity. The rhododendron grower needs only to know that pH 7 is the neutral point on a scale of 1 to 14. For every full point below pH 7, the acidity increases tenfold. Likewise, above pH 7, the alkalinity increases.

Ericaceae in general, and rhododendrons in particular, require a pH in the region of 4.5 to 5.5, but experiments have shown that a slightly higher pH, when caused by magnesium carbonate rather than calcium carbonate will produce no ill effects. On the other hand, contrary to what has been generally believed in the past, rhododendrons can suffer from too low a pH, at least where there is a deficiency of calcium. Working on the premise that 4.5 to 5.5 is a successful pH for the genus, a sample of soil should be analysed. This can be done either by a laboratory, or with a home soil-testing kit.

If a test shows that the soil has too high a pH (due to calcium) steps must be taken to reduce this to a working level. An application of ferrous sulphate at about 500 g/m^2 will reduce the pH by approximately one point on the pH scale (e.g. from 7.5 to 6.5). Flowers of sulphur is also commonly used to lower the pH, as is an annual dressing of a good acid peat.

MYCORRHIZAE

Mycorrhizae are fungi which live in close association with the roots of certain plants, either around the root, as in the case of beech trees, or within the root, as in most Ericaceae, including *Rhododendron*. The fungal hyphae take over the absorbing function of the root hairs, probably with greater efficiency.

As far as rhododendrons are concerned, it is accepted that this symbiotic relationship is beneficial to the plant, particularly where there is a nutrient deficiency in the soil, although some researchers claim that the presence of mycorrhizae is not essential. Nevertheless, a few growers consider it sufficiently important to inoculate soil in new plantations with mycorrhizae from established gardens.

If there are problems in establishing new rhododendron plants, this may be due to lack of mycorrhizae. This sometimes becomes apparent when a plant is transferred to the garden and is deprived of the supplementary feeding which it received in the nursery. Inoculation of the soil or increased feeding may well solve the problem.

Plants and Planting

Since the large scale move away from the old-fashioned nursery to the highly commercialised garden centre there has been a revolution in attitudes to selling plants. It was found that to sell trees and shrubs only during the dormant season, which has been the practice previously, was not a viable financial proposition. To enable plants to be sold throughout the year, the use of containers has become widespread. Growers must now supply garden centres with plants either already in containers or of a suitable size for putting in containers.

This supermarket-style of selling has mixed benefits for the purchaser for, while the more reputable garden centre offers, in containers, plants which have been properly treated, others are only interested in a quick turnover.

When purchasing rhododendrons, or any other shrub or tree, each plant should be examined carefully to determine whether or not it is potbound. This will be fairly obvious when it is knocked out of its pot or polyethylene bag. If it has been growing in one container for an excessively long time, the roots will have formed themselves into a tight hard mass and there will be no young feeding roots. It may, therefore, be very difficult to establish the specimen.

On the other hand, it is not uncommon to find plants for sale which have been in their containers for only 2 or 3 weeks. In this case, the roots will have had no opportunity to take hold in the new compost and, if the plants are removed from the containers, most of the soil will fall away. This may not be quite so important in autumn but, if the plant is purchased in summer, when conditions are dry, for immediate planting, the results could be disastrous.

With a few exceptions, the species and cultivars of *Rhododendron* obtainable at garden centres are only available in containers and choice is restricted to the popular sorts. However, one great advantage is that the rhododendrons can be purchased in full bloom and the flower type and colour are immediately obvious.

The enthusiast will undoubtedly wish to purchase some of the more uncommon species and cultivars. This can best be done through the specialist growers. Theoretically, young container-grown specimens can be planted at any time of the year. However, in specialist nurseries, the plants may be growing in open ground or in frames, in which case they will be available only from autumn until spring.

Once rhododendrons have become established and have produced a relatively large surface-rooting system, they become surprisingly easy to transplant. The best time for this operation is late summer or early autumn, when the young growth has hardened and the sap movement has slowed down.

If it is known well in advance that a large specimen has to be moved, certain steps can be taken to ensure the optimum chance of success. A trench must be taken out around the trunk, leaving a rootball as large as you can move with some assistance. Preferably, the diameter of the rootball should be equal to the height of the plant although this will not be possible with really large specimens. The trench should be dug and infilled with peat about a year in advance, so that any large roots which are cut will be encouraged to provide a young fibrous root system. The soil should be well watered within a week of transplanting if there is any indication of dryness at the root.

In theory, there is no limit to the size of plant which can be transplanted; the only restriction is the facilities available for handling the specimen. During the lifting operation, aim to preserve the maximum amount of soil around the root system in order to ensure the minimum amount of damage.

The bulk of the root system will be found within 30 cm of the surface and it is more important to concentrate on clearing this area of the rootball than to dig deeper. With large shrubs, this operation can take a considerable amount of time but it should not be rushed as the future establishment of the plant is at stake. Remove any peat from the trench before beginning the undercutting operation. When about one-third of the rootball has been undercut, assistance will be required to pull back the plant gently and allow the undercutting to proceed. Undercut until the approximate centre of the plant is reached. The procedure is then repeated on the opposite side of the rhododendron until the entire plant has been freed from the soil. If the specimen is too heavy to lift from the hole a series of skids and ropes can be employed to drag it free.

It has been known for a particularly large specimen to be left for as long as 1 month before replanting. This plant in fact suffered no harm from this extended period out of the soil, probably partly due to the very high rainfall experienced in the vicinity. This does show that, with a sufficiently large rootball, the success rate of transplanting large specimens should be very high.

USE OF ANTI-TRANSPIRANT SPRAYS

Anti-transpirant sprays can be applied to the foliage prior to lifting. These sprays are designed to reduce moisture loss while the root system is unable to supply the total water requirement of the plant. These sprays, which are milky white in appearance, are manufactured from a biodegradable plastic that breaks down slowly after application. Meanwhile the plant can send out new roots into the surrounding soil and become capable of supporting itself.

The manufacturer's instructions should be followed for the dilution of the concentrate with water; this is usually in the ratio of 1:4 respectively. The material should be applied by pressure sprayer but special care must be taken to wash all pipes and jets thoroughly after use.

PLANTING DISTANCES

The main factors governing planting distances and the position within a garden are the size of the shrub at planting time and the height and diameter that it will reach at maturity. The habit of the plant, i.e. whether it creeps along the ground, forms mounds, is narrow and straggly, large and dense or even epiphytic must also be taken into consideration, as should the benefit to the plant of the shelter provided by close planting. The nature of the area to be planted will also have an influence, i.e. whether it is a private garden, a botanic garden, estate or National Trust, or a local authority amenity area.

The smaller species and cultivars should be planted 3 m or more apart and the gaps should be interplanted with small bulbs and dwarf ground cover plants. These can be replaced by smaller plants or removed completely as the rhododendrons grow. In botanic gardens generally, numbers of a single species or cultivar are planted in large groups and, in this instance, where it is immaterial whether or not they merge, a closer spacing can be adopted. Local authorities invariably plant closely, both for immediate effect and to offset losses by vandalism and death of the plants. Transplanting can be undertaken should overcrowding occur. In the private garden, this sytem of planting is not generally adopted.

The medium to large species require a considerable amount of room as they may grow to as much as 5 m or more in diameter. One specimen of *R. falconeri*, at Glenarn, in Scotland, has reached a height of over 16 m.

Without a large garden, it is impossible to plant out specimens of the very big species into their final positions without interplanting with smaller species. This is an excellent system to adopt as the smaller species can be moved when the larger plants begin to crowd them out.

While not recommended for permanent positions, unless in a large garden, some members of the large-leaved series can be grown just for their foliage. They may have to be removed before reaching their full stature or before they are ready to flower, but nevertheless the pleasure derived will be ample reward. Other growers, with more room, will probably be quite willing to exchange a small specimen for a larger one.

PLANTING METHODS

There are four methods of planting commonly advocated.

In the first, which is most commonly used, the finished surface is level with the surrounding soil. A hole is taken out approximately one and a half times the depth and diameter of the existing rootball. The base of the hole should then be forked up to ensure that there is no hard, water-retentive layer below and a liberal quantity of an organic matter, such as peat or tree bark, should be put into the hole, together with some of the original soil. Enough soil should be returned to allow the top of the rootball to be flush with the ground surface when the plant is positioned in the hole (Fig. 1).

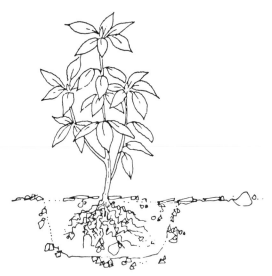

Fig. 1   Planting on level ground with average weather conditions.

The rhododendron can now be placed in position and the hessian or polypropylene root covering removed. If thin hessian sacking has been supplied with the plant, slitting the sides of the bag will be sufficient, as this material will soon rot down. Pieces of polyethylene must not be left in the hole since pockets of water can form and drainage can be impeded. With larger specimens, which have not been rootballed, the roots must be carefully spread out and any damaged portions cut back beyond the wound with a sharp pair of secateurs.

The original topsoil should now be backfilled around the roots and gently firmed. The firming operation must not be overdone or air will be excluded from the soil. The addition of a slow-release fertiliser, especially formulated for trees and shrubs, at $2.4\,\text{kg/m}^3$, is beneficial. A much better distribution will be achieved if the fertiliser is first mixed with four times its own weight of dry sand.

The second method of planting is often used where there is a danger of the soil retaining too much water during periods of heavy rainfall. The planting procedure is similar, but the hole is taken out to about the depth of the rootball only. The soil is then added so that, when the plant is in position, the root surface is approximately 10 cm above the surrounding soil level (Fig. 2). Sufficient topsoil is then added to completely cover the root system and the surface is then gently graded out with the back of a rake.

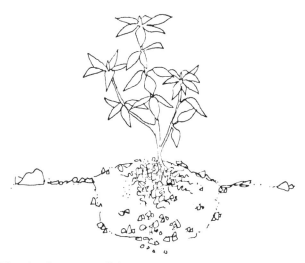

Fig. 2   Planting for wet conditions.

The third method is used where the rainfall is normally slightly low for the optimum growth of rhododendrons. Again the procedure is similar but the depth of the hole should be approximately twice that of the rootball. In this case the finished soil level is about 5 cm below that of the surrounding soil. The surface should then be graded out with the back of the rake to form a saucer-shaped depression, which will help to trap rainwater or water supplied from an irrigation system (Fig. 3). It is, however, important that drainage is adequate to cope with the occasional heavy downpour.

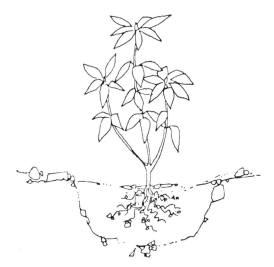

Fig. 3   Planting for dry conditions.

The final method, often used on slopes, is the excavation of a small plateau in which to set the plants. This will assist in trapping some of the rainwater which might normally run straight over the surface (Fig. 4). Good drainage, once again, is important.

WATERING-IN

It is advisable to water-in any spring- and summer-planted specimens with a fine rose. In the case of evergreen species in dry localities, this also may be necessary during autumn and winter.

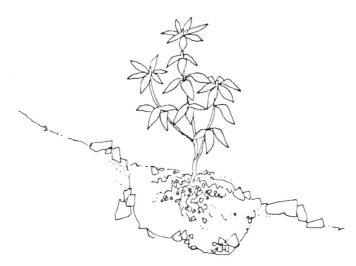

Fig. 4   Planting on a sloping site.

SUPPORTING THE PLANT

Large, top-heavy specimens will almost certainly require some form of support for 2 or 3 years after planting or transplanting. Tree stakes or similar supports (Fig. 5) are often recommended but unless you are fortunate enough to be in a sheltered area, with a good depth of soil into which the stake can be sunk, this method will not prove effective.

A safer if not quite so aesthetically pleasing method is to use guy wires. The diameter of the guy wire will depend on the size of specimen involved but multi-strand wire should be used for really large plants. Three iron or steel pegs are driven into the ground at equidistant points around the plant to form a triangle. These pegs should be slightly angled so that the point is towards the centre of the plant. A short piece of soft plastic or rubber hose is threaded over the guy wire which is then looped around the main stem or trunk of the rhododendron and tied back on itself. The other end is fixed to the peg and pulled tight (see Fig. 6). With large specimens, a radisseur or ratchet strainer can be used.

PROTECTION FROM ANIMALS

It is common on large estates to find wire mesh guards protecting specimen plants from hungry rabbits and deer. In recent years, since the

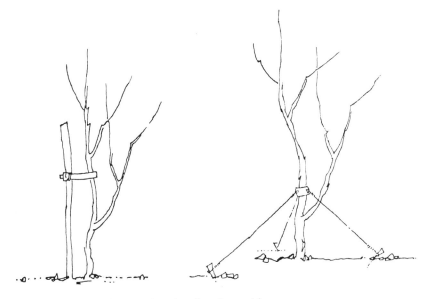

Fig. 5   (Left) Supporting the plant by staking.

Fig. 6   (Right) Supporting the plant with guy wires.

decline of myxomatosis, the number of rabbits has increased so much that they can be found in quite small town gardens. Deer, too, are increasing in numbers and any garden adjacent to large stretches of parkland might well be visited by some of these beautiful but unwelcome animals. If considered necessary, guards can be made by stretching chicken wire round 1.3 m stakes, which have been hammered into the ground. The bottom end of the wire should be buried 5 cm below ground level.

Irrigation

Irrigation is necessary either to make good any deficiencies of a normally adequate rainfall or to make cultivation possible in areas where the rainfall is totally inadequate. It is difficult to lay down a watering regime for rhododendrons, as the many species and cultivars, particularly when planted for ornamental effect, have different requirements and, moreover, they are generally grown together.

There are, however, certain broad principles which should be followed:

(a) the plants should never be allowed to dry out, especially in spring when young foliage and flowers are beginning to appear.

38

(b) excessive watering in late summer can discourage the formation of flower buds.

(c) neutral or alkaline tapwater should be avoided if possible.

(d) overhead spraying should only be carried out in strong sunshine if a continuous supply of water is guaranteed. Occasional overhead spraying can lead to scorch in very bright sunlight if no shade is available.

(e) when watering, ensure that sufficient water is applied to soak right down to the roots.

(f) do not apply the water in such a manner as to wash soil from the roots.

EQUIPMENT

Watering Cans The use of the watering can as a means of irrigation is limited to the small nursery, greenhouse or small private garden. It is worth investing in a good quality plastic or metal can which may be equipped with different types of roses. These can be purchased either with the can or separately as an extra. Cheap cans leak, produce drips where they are not wanted and will not stand up to the use which they will be put to over the years.

Hoses Since the advent of relatively cheap lightweight hoses, the older type of rubber hose has practically disappeared, even in commercial establishments. Within reason, purchase the most expensive type of plastic hose which you can afford. These hoses are reinforced to take mains pressure and will not kink or twist in the same way as cheaper hoses.

Another advantage is the range of watering accessories which can be fitted. These include quick-release couplings, adjustable nozzles, sprinklers, tap connectors and hose reels, all of which will prove to be a good investment for the serious horticulturist. Many of these enable the water supply to be cut off at the nozzle and, in a large garden, will save walking back to the tap, which might be a considerable distance away.

Permanent Watering Systems With the exception of golf courses and large commercial nurseries, few growers can afford or even need a permanent watering system. However, a garden tap, strategically placed, from which a hose can be run or a watering can filled, will prove invaluable.

WATER SUPPLIES

Pumped Supply Should you own a garden with a stream flowing through it, the use of a pumped supply in dry weather might be worth considering, providing that local by-laws permit it. The regulations surrounding the electrical wiring of pumps can be quite complex and it is worth seeking the advice of a specialist contractor.

Gravity-Fed Piped Supply   If you are lucky enough to have a large garden, on a hillside, with a stream, it may be possible to construct a small dam to which a plastic pipe can be attached. This system is quite common in Scotland, where the natural hilly terrain and numerous streams make this an economical and sensible way of obtaining water on the few occasions when it is needed.

Regulations Governing Water Supply   Regulations vary according to locality and the local water authority should be consulted before either connecting into mains supplies or drawing water from rivers.

Mulching

While irrigation is important when the plants are not receiving an adequate rainfall, mulching is equally important in conserving the rain which does fall. At the same time, it smothers any annual weed growth. The purpose of a mulch is to reduce the amount of water lost by evaporation from the soil surface. As a secondary benefit, mulching also slows down the rate of frost penetration into the soil, although, in the early part of the winter, the air temperature immediately above a mulch can be lower than that above bare soil. In hot climates, mulching keeps the roots cool during the summer.

While, commercially, polyethylene is being widely used to conserve moisture, especially in vegetable production, it is unlikely, principally for aesthetic reasons, that it will ever become popular in rhododendron plantations. The mulches used are almost universally organic and consist of materials such as peat, tree bark, leafmould, spruce needles and sawdust.

If finance, time and material permit, a mulch 25 mm deep should be applied every year to the smaller species and one about 75 mm deep to the larger species. If newly collected leaves are being used, double this amount will do no harm since there is a reduction of about 50% during the winter due to natural compaction and decay.

Autumn and early winter is the normal time of the year to apply mulches but if there is any indication of soil dryness, watering should be carried out prior to mulching.

At least one garden open to the public is so fastidious in its bid for tidiness that its staff rakes off every leaf that falls from the trees above the rhododendron plantation. In my opinion, this is not only time-consuming but totally detrimental to the well being of the plants and, consequently, considerable quantities of water need to be applied during the summer period. Paths are the only areas which need to be kept free of fallen leaves and this is mainly for the sake of safety. Spring-flowering bulbs, such as snowdrops and narcissi, will appear quite happily through 2.5–5 cm of fallen leaves.

Feeding

Plant physiologists have long been aware that a number of elements are essential for healthy plant growth. These elements are required in different amounts and will be described accordingly.

MAJOR ELEMENTS

Nitrogen Nitrogen is required mainly for the formation of proteins and the rapid extension of growth. An over-application of a nitrogenous fertiliser will lead to the production of soft sappy growth which is vulnerable to pests and diseases. As with any other shrub, it is important not to apply a dressing of nitrogen too late in the season because the young growth must be allowed to ripen before the onset of colder weather.

The nitrogen which is applied to plants is derived generally from potassium nitrate or from an ammonium salt. Experiments have shown that nitrogenous fertilisers derived from the ammonium salt are far more suitable for rhododendrons than those derived from potassium nitrate. It has been suggested that this difference is due to the nitrate raising the pH of the leaf whereas the ammonium salt has the opposite effect. The most readily available nitrogenous fertiliser for rhododendrons is ammonium sulphate. Many of the dry compound and liquid fertilisers have no information as to the source of nitrogen printed on their labels and this can be a problem.

Many nurserymen feel that slow-acting fertilisers tend to release their nitrogen too late in the season and this is true in sheltered positions. However, in a very exposed situation, the natural retarding effect of the cold winds slows the growth to such an extent that, without a long-term nitrogen source, shoot extension would be severely limited.

Phosphorus Phosphorus is essential for the formation of certain proteins and is also generally associated with the development of a good healthy root system, flower bud formation and the maturation process of the plant. Superphosphate, which contains 18–21% water-soluble phosphoric acid (P_2O_5), is probably the most common source of this element.

Potassium   Potassium is involved in the metabolism of carbohydrates. It plays an important part in the formation of seeds, fruits and the ripening of growth in the autumn. The latter confers resistance to damage by frost, pests and diseases. Sulphate of potash contains about 50% of the potassium nutrient and is normally considered to be the best pure source of this element.

Magnesium   Magnesium is an integral part of chlorophyll, the green pigment essential for photosynthesis, found in the leaves of all flowering plants, ferns, algae and seaweeds. Without magnesium, the foliage will turn pale yellow and exhibit typical symptoms of chlorosis.

Originally it was thought that magnesium was only required in very small amounts but, more recently, scientists have generally agreed that magnesium is needed in quantities approximately equal to that of phosphorus and about a hundred times that of the trace elements.

There is a complex relationship between magnesium and calcium which is still being studied, but it has been proved that a high pH alone will not necessarily cause magnesium to become unavailable. It is more likely that calcium, if present in excessive amounts (i.e. excessive for rhododendrons), will not only raise the pH but will also lock up any available magnesium, causing the plants to show signs of chlorosis. It should be noted that without analysis of both the leaf and the soil, it is difficult to tell exactly which deficiency is causing the problem.

If chlorosis develops, and if it is suspected that magnesium deficiency may be responsible, an application of Epsom salts (magnesium sulphate) as a foliar spray at the rate of 2 kg/100 l of water, plus wetting agent, may alleviate the problem. Foliar sprays are readily absorbed into the tissue of the leaf and the results should be fairly dramatic, but unless the cause is eliminated at the source, the symptoms will once again return. For more long-term effects a liquid feed of magnesium sulphate at the rate of 50 g/l diluted 1:200, should be applied to the soil in the spring.

MINOR ELEMENTS

Calcium   Among other functions, calcium plays an important role in the formation of the cell walls of all green plants. Calcium, however, is probably better known for its ability to counteract acidity and, as a rule, it is to be avoided in locations where members of the Ericaceae are planted.

For many years, it was assumed that the cause of failure of rhododendrons in certain soils was due to a high pH alone. However, in the 1950s, Dr Tod of Edinburgh carried out experiments to ascertain whether these failures were caused by the alkalinity of the soil, the toxic action of calcium, or by a deficiency of another element induced by an excess of calcium. The results showed that, where the pH was raised by the addition of calcium, definite adverse effects became apparent. It was, nevertheless, more complicated than a simple dislike for excessive calcium, for various other elements, such as magnesium, manganese and iron, can be locked up and made unavailable, due to the presence of calcium in anything other than very small quantities. In one experiment ground limestone cured the problem. It should be pointed out that this is an unusual occurrence and growers would be well advised to check out the other more likely causes of chlorosis before applying lime in any form. More recent experiments have indicated that, at a pH of 3.3–3.9 in certain soils, and possibly in areas of high rainfall, there can be such low levels of calcium present that chlorosis can occur due to a shortage of this element.

The term *calcifuge* is applied to plants, most noticeably the Ericaceae, which dislike calcium, but the truth of the matter may well be that they can assimilate calcium at such a rate from soils which are normally relatively low in this material, that they themselves are the basic cause of the problem.

Manganese Manganese is necessary for the formation of chlorophyll and for respiration and protein synthesis. Like iron, it is required only in very small quantities, but nevertheless it must be available to the plant. Current thinking seems to indicate that chlorosis due to manganese deficiency alone is less common than was previously supposed, but this has not yet been confirmed absolutely.

Iron Although iron is utilised in the young growing tips of most plants, it also acts as a catalyst during the photosynthetic process. A lot of publicity over the years has suggested that iron deficiency, resulting from lime in the soil, was the principal cause of chlorosis in the genus *Rhododendron,* although deficiencies of other elements, particularly magnesium, but also manganese and even calcium, can cause considerable chlorosis.

While iron is normally present in fairly large quantities, many physiologists working in this field believe that it becomes unavailable to the plant under high pH conditions. Even the iron which has been present in the tissues is thrown out of its soluble form in the cell sap by the presence of added calcium.

The addition of ferrous sulphate will increase the acidity of the soil, and reduce chlorosis by making the iron available once again. Chelated iron or sequestrene has been used quite successfully over many years as a temporary answer to the problem but since this material contains a fairly high proportion of magnesium as well as iron, the true cause of the chlorosis might well have been masked.

Sulphur Sulphur plays an important role in the formation of amino acids and proteins, and its absence will restrict growth and cause a yellowing of the foliage. The element itself comes in many forms, the most common of which is the bright yellow powder known as flowers of sulphur.

Flowers of sulphur is more frequently used to counteract the alkalinity of a soil, rather than as a means of supplying the element to a given plant. Ferrous sulphate is a safer form of application, although it is seldom that a sulphur deficiency in itself constitutes a problem in industrialised areas with a high level of pollution. Many fertilisers, such as sulphate of potash and sulphate of ammonia, contain this element in the form of a salt.

TRACE ELEMENTS

Boron, molybdenum, zinc and copper are the most important trace elements and they all play a part in the metabolism of the plant although they do not normally turn up as deficiencies in rhododendrons. These, plus other trace elements, must, however, be added to any compost where the soil fraction has been omitted. They can be purchased in a form known as fritted trace elements (FTE). The standard rate of application of FTE for soil-less composts is 390 g/m³.

Pest and Disease Control

Because *Azalea* is now part of the genus *Rhododendron*, and is subject to the same pests and diseases, it will not be considered separately for the purposes of this chapter.

It should be appreciated that the establishment of healthy growth should be the first objective, as a healthy plant is much better able to withstand attacks by pest and disease and also competition with weeds. Once this is achieved, chemical plant protection can be considered.

Physiological Disorders

One of the most common symptoms of physiological disorder in plants is chlorosis. This is the yellowing of parts of the plant that are normally green and is the result of lack of chlorophyll formation. There are many causes of chlorosis in *Rhododendron,* the most common being a lack of available iron, but nitrogen, magnesium or even calcium deficiency may also be responsible.

IRON DEFICIENCY

Iron is normally found in ample quantities in the soil but can become unavailable to the plant because of a change in pH level. Iron will even enter the leaves of the plant, but remain insoluble, and hence unavailable, because the soil sap is not sufficiently acid.

Symptoms The main symptom is a change in the colour of the foliage from green to a sickly yellow or white with a mottled effect. The whole plant becomes chlorotic and, if the deficiency is not made good, the plant will gradually die.

Control A fast but temporary means of control is to spray the foliage with a chelated iron compound; this will remain available to the plant as it passes through the cuticle and into the cell sap. More permanent methods are either to add the chelated iron to the soil at 120–150 g in 30 l of water/10 m^2 or to bring the pH down to a level of 4.5–5 by adding ferrous sulphate or flowers of sulphur.

45

NITROGEN DEFICIENCY

This often results from soil micro-organisms utilising free nitrogen in the soil to break down organic matter, which is normally abundant in *Rhododendron* habitats. The nitrogen thus becomes unavailable to the plant.

Symptoms The leaves become yellowish green in colour and new foliage fails to develop to its full size. The centres of the leaves remain green longer but the contrast of colour is not so marked as that found in iron deficiency chlorosis.

Control This is achieved either by the addition of sulphate of ammonia to the soil or by high nitrogen foliar feeds during the growing season. Sulphate of ammonia also has the secondary beneficial effect of reducing the pH level. Materials such as fresh sawdust should not be used as a mulch in cases of nitrogen deficiency.

POTASSIUM DEFICIENCY

Symptoms Dead areas appear on the foliage and there is inter-vascular yellowing and scorching at the leaf tips and edges; the leaves eventually turn a bronze colour. New foliage remains small and stunted and the flower quality is poor.

Control As a long-term measure sulphate of potash should be added to the soil. For temporary control, a high potassium foliar spray should be used during the growing season.

PHOSPHORUS DEFICIENCY

Symptoms This deficiency is marked by the appearance of reddish purple blotches near the mid-rib on the underside of the leaf; this later spreads to the upper surface. The lower leaves turn brown and there is premature leaf fall. The flower colour is also generally poor.

Control A superphosphate or ammonium phosphate should be applied to the soil during the growing season.

MAGNESIUM DEFICIENCY

Symptoms The plants become chlorotic and reddish purple blotches appear on the upper leaves; older leaves become bronzed, curl downwards and/or die at the tip. There is premature leaf fall and the flowers are generally small.

Control   A simple but effective temporary expedient is to spray the plant with magnesium sulphate at the rate of 8 kg/100 l water. For a long-term effect, magnesium sulphate should be applied to the soil at a rate of 1 kg/20m².

WATERLOGGING

Symptoms   Although rhododendrons require a plentiful supply of water they will not tolerate stagnant conditions. Lack of air at the roots will cause the death of root hairs and, in winter, when the plant is still transpiring, there will be a sudden wilting, followed by death of the plant, unless it can manufacture new roots quickly. These symptoms should not be confused with those of frost damage.
Control   Drainage should be improved by the construction of raised beds, improvement of the soil or by the installation of drains.

DROUGHT

Symptoms   Rhododendrons make their best growth in areas of high rainfall. In drought conditions their natural defences, such as waxy leaves, scales and the rolling action of the leaf, will help to conserve moisture. However, after an extended period of drought, there will be permanent damage.
Control   The genus is principally surface-rooting, therefore any action which can be taken to keep the roots cool and moist will be a decided advantage, e.g. a mulch with peat and leafmould or crushed tree bark.

SUN SCALD

Symptoms   Sun scald, which sometimes looks like a disease because it is often followed by a fungal attack, appears as a disfiguring and brown spotting of the leaf tips and edges. It can occur in both summer and winter. In winter, brown patches appear on either side of the mid-rib when the leaf is curled up in cold weather.
Control   The best method of control is by natural protection. This can be best effected by positioning the plant in the shade of larger trees or shrubs. (Excessive shade, however, will result in poor flower bud formation.)

Symptoms   The extent of damage will be determined by the stage of development reached by the plant, when the frosts occur. Because of the wide range of flowering times (January to July and August to December in the northern and southern hemispheres respectively), the flowers of the earlier species and cultivars can be badly damaged by late spring frosts and the foliage by low temperatures in early autumn or spring.

The deciduous types are hardy in bud and, even when the early flowering species are just showing colour, little damage will result from a light frosting. The foliage, however, begins its growth cycle at the first sign of a mild spell in early spring and this is when damage can occur, as the unfurling leaves are too soft to withstand extreme cold followed by the bright sunlight. The flowers of evergreen species and cultivars are frequently damaged and, in the case of the later starters, any immature foliage can suffer badly from an early autumn frost.

In very severe weather conditions, splitting of the bark may occur (Fig. 7) and this can leave an open wound which allows the entry of fungi and other pathogens.

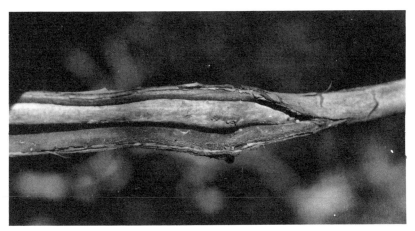

Fig. 7   Bark split.

Control   Apart from physically sheltering the plant with screens made from hessian or plastic materials, or with branches of conifers, the only other remedy concerns the culture of the plant. The restriction of water and of nitrogenous fertiliser in late autumn will help to produce a reasonably hardy plant.

48

RAIN DAMAGE

Symptoms Normally this will occur only on the flowers. The damage which appears after heavy rain showers is seen as small brown spots on the petals and there is very little which can be done to prevent this. Rain can also cause wounds on the petals which leave them open to fungal attack.

Control Where the blooms are being grown for exhibition some form of artificial protection, such as polyethylene sheeting, may be employed.

SNOW DAMAGE

Symptoms Snow may cause considerable damage, particularly in the case of the large-leaved species, where its weight in a heavy fall can cause the whole branch to bend over and break. This will leave the plant open to a secondary attack by fungi.

Control Short of manually clearing the snow, or judicious pruning of weak branches, there is very little action which can be taken to prevent some damage occurring.

Fungal Diseases

RHODODENDRON WILT, ROOT ROT (*Phytophthora cinnamomi*)

Rhododendron wilt or root rot usually attacks young plants, but older specimens too can be infected. The mode of attack is through the roots.

Symptoms It can be seen as a wilt, which appears not only in warm conditions, but also in cool damp weather. The leaves have an olive-green cast and, if the bark is scraped away from the stem, it will appear brown and dead near the base.

Control There is no cure and any infected plants should be dug up and burnt. The soil where the infected plant has been growing, and the surrounding area, should be watered with maneb, zineb, nabam or mancozeb.

By lowering the pH value from about 5 to 4 it is possible to gain some control over the disease as a low pH does not favour its spread. A severe winter will also reduce the spread of the fungus in the following year, as the mycelium cannot normally withstand freezing temperatures.

Since the pathogen can survive in the tissues of dead rhododendrons it is good cultural practice to remove any debris from the area surrounding infected plants. It is worth noting that a garden may contain alternative hosts, such as yew, heather and certain conifers.

HONEY FUNGUS (*Armillaria mellea*)

This is a very common and serious pathogen, which attacks almost every tree and shrub, including rhododendrons. Where there is an infection in a large plantation, the consequences can be extremely serious.

Symptoms Honey fungus will cause a yellowing and premature fall of the foliage, which, in the case of evergreen species, will probably occur during the summer. There is a softening and blackening of the stem and, often, a chalky white mycelium is present, as well as a mushroom-like smell of decay from the bark. The later stages of fungal growth will show leathery black, bootlace-like rhizomorphs between the bark and the xylem.

Control By the rhizomorph stage, it is too late to do anything but dig out the infected plant and burn it. It is also important to remove as much as possible of the old root system from the surrounding soil as this is a potential source of reinfection. The ground should then be treated with a soil sterilant, such as formaldehyde in a 2% solution. All other debris in the area, e.g. tree stumps and branches, must be removed and burnt. If possible, it is best not to replant an infected area with trees or shrubs for a period of 4 or 5 years, to ensure that the soil is free of the fungus.

CROWN GALL (*Agrobacterium radiobacter* var. *tumefaciens*)

This is a bacterial disease which affects a wide range of plant species, including rhododendrons.

Symptoms Crown gall is an enlarged tumour-like growth which sometimes appears at a point near the soil level, where there has been an injury to the main stem. It looks like callus tissue and is quite hard to the touch.

Control Good hygiene is the main control used against this infection, which generally causes little harm to the plant. Careful inspection of the shrub before planting must be the principal defence, since there is a risk of infecting healthy stock by soil contamination should a wound occur. One other possible method of control, where chemical regulations permit, is the disinfection of the wound with 1% solution of an organo-mercury fungicide.

RHODODENDRON BLIGHT (*Phytophthora cactorum*)

The pathogen enters the plant through the leaf margins, twigs, old bloom stems and seed capsules.

Symptoms   Brown areas appear, followed by a silvery discoloration of the foliage, which then starts to curl and take on a withered appearance. Blight occurs initially on young wood and is typified by brown markings which encircle the stem where the infection has entered. The spread will be from the infected branch towards the main trunk and, if not halted, infection of the entire plant can take place.

Control   The most effective control is the removal of the infected branches and the painting of all cut surfaces with a copper fungicide and bitumenous compound. Bordeaux or Burgundy mix can be watered into the soil to eliminate any spores which might be present.

BOTRYTIS (*Botrytis* sp.)

Botrytis occurs on both outdoor and indoor plants, although it is more common indoors as it thrives in excess humidity, low temperatures and inadequate ventilation. Both seedlings and mature plants are attacked. Entry of the fungus is normally through a wound scar. The *Botrytis* spores can easily be spread in air currents, although considerable reinfection occurs because the mycelium can overwinter as a saprophyte on dead plant material.

Symptoms   The infected parts of the plant become covered in a grey powdery mould.

Control   Indoors, the main method of control is to decrease the humidity by providing adequate ventilation and raising the temperature. Where seedlings have been attacked, the plant density should be reduced.

Outdoors, drainage plays an important part. If possible, avoid planting in poorly drained ground or, alternatively, improve the soil conditions to provide a more open medium.

Once infected, all plant material should be burnt.

Chemical controls should be the last resort, since prevention is better than cure. Any wounds which occur should be painted with dichloran paste and the cut surface should be coated with a bituminous compound to prevent entry of fungal spores. Plants growing inside can be fumigated with technazene. Whether indoors or outdoors, the plants can be sprayed with thiram or benomyl.

DAMPING-OFF (*Pythium* and Other Genera)

Rhododendrons are no different from most other plants at the seedling stage. They should germinate within 3 or 4 weeks of sowing, provided that the seed is fresh and is sown under the correct conditions. If the seed is sown in unsterilised soil or sown too thickly or if the humidity is too high, there is every likelihood that the seedlings will suffer from damping-off.

Symptoms The stems become narrow and pinched at or just above soil level. The seedlings look slightly wilted although, because of their size, it is difficult to see this. Quite soon the seedling topples over and dies, sometimes becoming slightly reddish in colour.

Control The main control of damping-off is cultural. Shredded sphagnum moss is an ideal seed-sowing medium since it is extremely free-draining, providing it has not been compacted, while at the same time it holds sufficient moisture to provide a constant supply of water without daily attention.

Chemical control can be in the form of a seed-dressing, a dusting of captan or thiram before sowing. The allied disease, stem rot, produced by the damping-off fungus, *Rhizoctonia*, can cause damage to the roots of older plants.

BUD BLAST (*Pycnosteanus azaleae*)

This pathogen is thought to be spread by the female leaf-hopper, which makes incisions in the bud during egg-laying.   •

Symptoms The fungus attacks the flower buds, making them first turn brown and then fail to open. The bud then becomes covered with a multitude of fine black bristles, which are the spore-producing bodies.

Control Mechanical control is by the removal of the infected buds. This, however, is not practical on a large scale.

Bud blast may be controlled chemically by spraying with a fungicide, such as Bordeaux mixture, during the summer and autumn. It is, however, also advisable to kill the leaf-hopper by spraying with gamma-HCH or malathion in August (or January in the southern hemisphere).

LEAF SPOT (*Exobasidium sp.*)

This is not a very important disease in rhododendrons.

Symptoms Leaf spot starts as small yellow spots on the leaf. These eventually turn brown.

Control Where it is deemed necessary, control can be achieved by spraying the infected plants with thiram.

LEAF SCORCH (*Septoria solidaris*)

Leaf scorch can occur in areas of very high humidity.

Symptoms   Small round spots with a faintly yellow covering appear on the foliage.

Control   Chemical control with a spray, such as maneb, can be effective or hand-pick and burn the old fallen foliage.

RUST (Various Species)

This fungal pathogen is not a serious problem in rhododendrons, although it does sometimes occur locally in spring and early summer.

Symptoms   Small orange pustules appear on the underside of the leaf. These later become powdery as the fungus matures.

Control   It can normally be controlled by applying a foliar spray of mancozeb, particularly on the underside of the leaf.

POWDERY MILDEW (*Microsphaera alni*)

This fungus, one of the several powdery mildews, is an exception to the rule that cool damp conditions are necessary for the spread of fungal diseases. In this particular case, the powdery mildew thrives in a dry climate and serious attacks only become prevalent in hot weather. It can, therefore, be seen that, since *Rhododendron* as a genus prefers cooler, damper conditions, the majority of growers will not experience great difficulties with this pathogen.

Symptoms   The disease can appear on the stem, leaves and the flowers as a superficial powdery growth during the summer months. Later, the white powdery mats will turn brown.

Control   Benomyl or dinocap should prove effective against this pathogen.

LEAF GALL (*Exobasidium vaccinii*)

This strange-looking growth (Fig. 8) is caused by a fungus, *Exobasidium vaccinii*, which is introduced by a bacterium. It is fairly common on cultivars of the greenhouse azalea, *R. simsii*, but can also be seen on very small hardy species.

Symptoms   It appears as a malformation of the foliage which becomes thickened and hard with fleshy protuberances. The surface is initially waxy, but later becomes covered with masses of white fungal spores.

Control   The infected tissues can be removed by hand or, if the outbreak is serious, a foliar spray of zineb can be employed.

Fig. 8   Leaf gall (Exobasidium vaccinii) *on* R. ferrugineum.

WITCHES' BROOM (*Exobasidium vaccinii-uliginosii*)

This occurs very occasionally and is found more frequently on *Betula* species.

Symptoms   An unmistakable abnormal profusion of short twiggy branches.

Control   Remove and burn the infected branches.

Insects and Allied Pests

RHODODENDRON BUG (*Stephanitis rhododendri*)

The rhododendron bug is a shiny, yellowish to dark brown insect, approximately 3–4 mm long, which feeds in groups on the underside of the leaves. The adult has broad lace-like wings, from which its other common name, lace bug, is derived. The nymphs, if viewed under a magnifying glass, can be seen to be covered in small brown spines.

Symptoms Although both adults and nymphs feed on the underside of the leaf, the damage initially shows up mainly on the top surface as yellowing of the foliage. Eventually the entire leaf will turn yellow and die while the underside becomes spotted by the insect's sticky excrement. In addition, the eggs are laid in slots cut in the main leaf veins, and these show brown lesions as a result.

Control Where an attack is mild or where there are only a few rhododendrons growing in the vicinity, hand-picking and burning of the infected foliage is possible. However, where larger areas of rhododendrons are infected, control can be effected by spraying the underside of the leaves with malathion or gamma-HCH solution. Two applications should be made at 2- to 3-week intervals as soon as the insects are seen hatching from the overwintered eggs in early summer. A nicotine spray is highly effective if applied on still days and at a temperature above 16°C. It has been reported that plants growing in full sun seem to be more troubled by this insect, therefore the provision of light shade can be an advantage.

RHODODENDRON LEAF-HOPPER (*Graphocephala coccinea*)

The leaf-hopper is an insect, approximately 9 mm long, with blue, red and yellow striped markings. It spread from the United States of America to Europe in the 1930s and is known to increase the spread of the fungal disease known as bud blast (which may also occur in the absence of the pest).

Symptoms Most reports indicate that the actual damage caused by the leaf-hopper is negligible. Despite this the link with bud blast indicates that measures should be taken to eliminate this probable carrier.

Control If bud blast becomes a problem, chemical control of the leaf-hopper can be effected by spraying with malathion, gamma-HCH or nicotine. Dimethoate, a systemic insecticide, can also be used.

RHODODENDRON WHITEFLY (*Dialeurodes   chittendenii*);
AZALEA WHITEFLY (*Dealius azaleae*)
Whiteflies are more generally associated with greenhouse crops, but certain species can be found on rhododendrons, especially in the warmer climates. The adult is unmistakable, although individual species are not easily distinguished without a magnifying glass. They are approximately triangular in shape, 1.25 mm long, with powdery white wings. Whitefly adults cluster on the underside of the foliage near the growing tips and, when disturbed, flutter about in great numbers. The nymphs are small, flattened and oval.

Symptoms   This pest causes damage in two ways. Firstly, and most obvious, is the yellow mottling of the foliage, which, if allowed to go unchecked, will lead to the distortion and eventual death of the growing tip. Secondly there is the build-up of the honeydew-like secretion which encourages the growth of a sooty mould. This prevents light reaching the leaves, thus stopping photosynthesis.

Control   Spray the undersides of the leaves with malathion, gamma-HCH or permethrin at 14-day intervals, as soon as the adults are seen.

RED SPIDER MITE (*Tetranychus urticae*)

The red spider mite is just visible to the naked eye, approximately 0.5 mm long, and yellow with black spots. In the autumn, this pest turns red before going into hibernation. This pest, like whitefly, is best known for its attack on greenhouse crops. However, during the periods of dry warm weather, it can become a nuisance outdoors and, because of its high rate of reproduction, can cause severe damage quite quickly.

Symptoms   The foliage becomes mottled and yellow in colour, eventually turning bronze. A very fine webbing usually covers the young growing shoot, which then stops growing and may die. In severe infestations, masses of mites will collect at the tips of the growing points and are then easily picked up on clothing and spread to other plants.

Control   There are two main forms of control. The most common method, employed by both the amateur and the professional, is the chemical spray. Potted azaleas are most effectively treated by dipping them into the spray solution. Unfortunately, where chemicals are frequently used, resistant strains of mites will eventually occur. It is, therefore, advisable to vary the treatment to prevent this happening.

The following chemicals have all been proved to work quite well but care must be exercised. Tetradifon is used for the control of the eggs and the young active stage. It is also available as a fumigant smoke for use under glass. Dimethoate is a systemic insecticide which has proved effective against many pests, but it should be used with caution as certain species of *Rhododendron* may show susceptibility. Dicofol, kills all stages of the mite and should be sprayed in midsummer. A mixture of dicofol and tetradifon can be used to reduce the chances of resistance. Malathion, effective against the active stages, may be sprayed at 21-day intervals. Derris, is effective against the active stages, but will probably require several applications. Where the standard materials fail, a spray of white oil emulsion (leafshine material or 'spraying oil'), is a suitable alternative.

An alternative is biological control. Commercially, the use of the Chilean predatory mite, *Phytoseiulus persimilis*, has found much favour, especially on greenhouse crops. It is little used by the amateur, but despite this, any gardener who is looking after large numbers of plants might be well advised to investigate this method of control. It should be noted that this mite cannot be used in conjuction with insecticides and some fungicides. Suppliers of the predator mite usually provide lists of compatible materials.

WEEVILS

Three species are commonly responsible for damage to rhododendrons, both indoors and outdoors. These are the vine weevil (*Otiorhynchus sulcatus*), the clay-coloured weevil (*O. singularis*) and the leaf weevil (*Phyllobius* spp.).

The adult vine weevil is a wingless beetle, approximately 8 mm long and dull black in colour, with small patches of yellow scales just visible to the naked eye. The adult clay-coloured weevil is similar but slightly smaller, 6–8 mm long, and brown with lighter speckled markings which, under magnification, can be seen to consist of scales arranged in groups like flower petals. The adult leaf weevil is 6–8 mm long and green or brown with a silvery or bronzy appearance, depending on the species.

The larvae of all these species are similar in appearance, being legless with a curved, fleshy, whitish body and brown head.

Symptoms All three species cause a similar type of damage. The adults gnaw the bark of the young shoots and flower stems and this causes a sudden collapse of the affected part. However, the most noticeable damage is that of the notched holes in the foliage (Fig. 9), an almost unmistakable symptom of attack in rhododendrons.

Fig. 9   Weevil damage.

The larvae feed in the soil on the roots of many plants, but the most frequent cause for concern is pot plants in the greenhouse. It is in such conditions that the *R. simsii* group are frequently grown. A bad infestation will result in the entire plant showing wilt symptoms, even when it has never been allowed to dry out. This invariably results in death unless corrective measures are taken early enough.

Control of Adults   This can be either chemical or mechanical. The adults appear to be relatively resistant to most chemicals, but gamma-HCH applied to the foliage and soil as a dust or spray has given some measure of control. Since these insects are really only active at night, and spend most of the daylight hours in crevices in the soil, it is difficult to ensure direct contact between the weevil and the insecticide unless a thorough soil drench is applied.

Another method of control which has been tried against wingless weevils is the use of grease-bands around the stems of the plants. This is only effective if applied to all the plants in an area because, although the weevils cannot fly, they can move from plant to plant by leaf or branch contact.

Mechanical control can be achieved by trapping the insects. The provision of hiding places for the insects during the day, e.g. corrugated paper around the bottom of the plants, which can then be removed, has proved effective on a small scale. Another very simple method is to place a white sheet around the base of the plant in the late afternoon or early evening and to shake the plants vigorously. The weevils, if present, will fall on to the sheet where they can easily be spotted and disposed of in a jar of paraffin.

Control of Larvae Incorporation of a dust of gamma-HCH or a soil drench of the liquid formulation gives moderate control providing it is carried out efficiently. Where damage to the roots occurs on older specimens, the problem is compounded by the difficulty of ensuring that the chemical reaches the centre of the rootball where the larvae are working. In this situation a hole should be made carefully with a pole and the insecticide poured in; the surrounding area should then be watered thoroughly with a solution of insecticide.

AZALEA LEAF-MINER (*Caloptilia azaleela*)

There are many species of leaf-mining caterpillar which attack various plants. The azalea leaf-miner favours mainly the *R. simsii* cultivars (the greenhouse azalea) under glass, although it has been found outdoors. Initially, the caterpillar is legless and almost transparent; later it develops legs and turns yellowish green.

Symptoms There are two main signs of damage. One is the appearance on the leaf of a thin twisting line which eventually turns brown; the other is a blister near the mid rib, where more than one caterpillar is feeding. This blister eventually turns brown and, in severe cases, the leaf may die and drop off.

Control The leaf-miner may be controlled by spraying at 10- to 14-day intervals with malathion, diazinon or gamma-HCH. The alternative method, of handpicking or crushing the insect within the leaf, may be used where only a few plants are involved.

TORTRIX MOTHS

Leaf-tying or tortrix moths including *Ditula angustiorana*, *Archips rosana* and *Tortrix viridana*. The tortrix moths are a fairly large group of insects which damage a wide range of ornamental and commercial trees and shrubs, including *Rhododendron*. The caterpillars, which are green or greenish yellow, cause most of the damage during early to midsummer.

Symptoms The damage varies according to species. Some feed on the foliage of the rhododendron and cut irregular holes, while other species, such as *D. angustiorana,* tie the leaves together with silky threads; still others roll the individual leaf to use as a refuge during the winter.

Control Unless there is a large-scale attack, the use of chemicals as a means of control should be avoided because it is extremely difficult to ensure that the spray is actually reaching the species which curl the foliage. If the caterpillar is noticed at an early stage, the normal methods, such as high-volume spraying of carbaryl, derris, or trichlorphon can be carried out. As with all chemicals, the susceptibility of many species of *Rhododendron* is not known, therefore trial sprays should be carried out first. In small attacks, hand-picking and burning is a safe effective method.

RHODODENDRON BORER (*Sesia rhododendri*)

This pest is not yet known in the British Isles and is one of a group of caterpillars which damages many ornamental shrubs, including *Rhododendron.* The larvae are approximately 18 mm long and white with a brown head.

Symptoms The caterpillar tunnels its way around the stem just below the bark, throwing out sawdust which can be found at the base of the trunk. This, interrupts the passage of nutrients and water through the plant, thus causing the sudden death of an entire section of the branch.

Control The only practical method of control is to kill the adult female when it is laying eggs, normally in midsummer, by spraying with gamma-HCH or malathion. It is also important to remove and burn the infected branches as close to the main stem as possible.

LEOPARD MOTH (*Zeuzera pyrina*)

The leopard moth caterpillar is a common species of stem borer affecting *Rhododendron.* The caterpillar is approximately 50 mm long, yellowish white in colour, with black spots and a brownish head.

Symptoms The caterpillar tunnels into the wood of smaller branches causing wilting of the foliage. If this is severe the entire branch will die.

Control At an early stage it is possible to insert a piece of florist's wire into the tunnel and pierce the caterpillar. Alternatively a syringe can be used to inject a solution of gamma-HCH into the tunnels. The entrance can then be blocked with putty. Removal of badly infected branches will reduce the caterpillar population.

WINTER MOTH (*Operophtera brumata*)

The winter moth is a common defoliator in parks and gardens.

Symptoms   The green 'looper' caterpillar of the winter moth feeds inside a tube of top leaves bound together with silk (like tortrices).

Control   On deciduous plants, the pest can be controlled by winter washes which kill the eggs. Alternatively, tree-banding grease can be applied to the stems in autumn, to prevent the wingless adult female moths from climbing up to lay eggs. An early spray with carbaryl, derris, malathion or trichlorphon should also prove effective.

VAPOURER MOTH (*Orgyia antigua*)

The caterpillars, which are 2.5 cm long, can be recognised by their markings of red, black, yellow and violet and the four tufts of yellow hair on the back.

Symptoms   This is common in gardens in the south of the British Isles where the caterpillar defoliates many species of shrubs, including rhododendrons.

Control   Control is identical to that for the winter moth.

RHODODENDRON APHID (*Masonaphis lambersi*)

The rhododendron aphid was first found in England and the Netherlands in 1971, attacking evergreen species and cultivars. This aphid was probably spread from the United States of America where it was first described in 1960. There are three colour forms: dark red, green or yellow.

Symptoms   The aphid attacks the young leaves and disfigures them by distortion. The cast skins and exudations encourage the growth of sooty mould.

Control   Rhododendron aphid can be controlled by spraying with pirimicarb or other systemic insecticides.

AZALEA APHID (*Masonaphis azaleae*)

The azalea aphid is an infrequent but serious pest of deciduous and indoor azaleas. It is very similar in appearance to the rhododendron aphid.

Symptoms   The symptoms are similar to those caused by the rhododendron aphid.

Control   Control methods are identical to those for the rhododendron aphid.

Rhododendron, in common with many other trees and shrubs, can suffer from mosses and lichens (Fig. 10). Lichens are a sign of a clean atmosphere and are seldom, if ever, seen growing to any harmful extent in polluted city atmospheres.

Fig. 10   Lichen.

Control   In deciduous species, the eradication of the lichen with tar or petroleum oil and DNOC is not too difficult, providing the shrub is completely dormant. However, because of their high phytotoxicity, these compounds canot be used on any of the evergreen species. The KURUME section of the former Azalea series is particularly susceptible to lichen when the plants are older and one solution is to remove plants over 15 years old and replace them with new stock.

Although there appears to be very little evidence of trials being carried out with this particular problem in mind, a dusting with sulphur powder may well be worth trying.

Propagation

Propagation in its most general sense simply means the increase or multiplication of living things by natural means. In plants, this is achieved by sexual or asexual means.

Sexual production depends on the successful fertilisation of a female gamete by a male gamete to produce a seed. The male gametes are carried in the pollen grains, which are produced in the stamens of the flower; the female equivalent is the ovule, which develops in the ovary (Fig. 11).

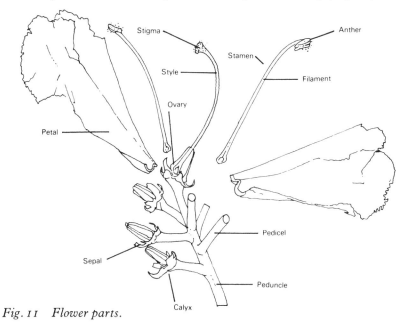

Fig. 11   Flower parts.

Fertilisation should not be confused with pollination, which is merely the transference of pollen from the anther of the stamen to the stigma of the ovary. Pollination is generally effected by insects, birds, small animals and wind although, in horticulture, it is often controlled by man to maintain or diversify species and varieties.

Asexual (vegetative) reproduction, or propagation in its narrower sense, occurs when part of a plant becomes separated from the main body of the parent and grows into a new plant. In horticulture, budding, grafting, layering and the use of cuttings are all extensions of this method of reproduction.

Aims and Purposes of Artificial Propagation

From a commercial standpoint, the artificial propagation of plants is a means of earning money, although, no doubt, the professional nurseryman might well offer many other reasons. Within the last 50 years, there have been many books written solely on propagation but the principles, if not the scientific knowledge, were known to the very first caveman who stepped forth and sowed a few seeds in a clearing to provide corn for his family in the winter.

Today, the simple reason why any non-food commercial plant grower is in business is to satisfy a demand from a public which has found a great deal of pleasure in the cultivation of ornamental plants.

Among the ornamental plant specialists, there are several groups involved in propagation and this has led to the modification of similar techniques to suit individual needs. These groups can be broadly categorised as: research units, commercial nurserymen, botanical gardens, National Trusts or similar bodies and amateur growers, both large and small.

THE RESEARCH UNIT

The research unit may be part of a government research station or a botanical garden, or even a professional grower who wishes to investigate a particular aspect of his existing method of propagation. Experiments into propagation may be made as a result of an enquiry from a grower who wants to increase his productivity or simply as a means of filling a gap in existing knowledge. The results are normally published in a bulletin from the relevant body.

THE COMMERCIAL NURSERYMAN

The commercial nurseryman has to run his nursery as a business and thus maintain its viability by making a profit. It is therefore important that the methods of propagation employed are cost-effective. It is only natural that there will be a limit to the range of species or cultivars which can be

SPECIES FOR THE SMALL GARDEN
1 *R. burmanicum*

2 *R. burmanicum*

3 *R. calostrotum*

4 *R. campylogynum*

5 *R. ciliatum*

6 *R. impeditum*

7 *R. ferrugineum*

8 *R. leucaspis*

9 *R. moupinense*

10 *R. racemosum*

11 *R. russatum*

12 *R. sperabile*

13 *R. wasonii*

SPECIES FOR THE MEDIUM-SIZED GARDEN
14 *R. balfourianum*

15 *R. bureavii*

16 *R. campylocarpum* var. *elatum*

17 *R. campylocarpum* var. *elatum*

18 *R. cinnabarinum* var. *purpurellum*

19 *R. cinnabarinum* var. *roylei* 'Magnificum'

20 *R. davidsonianum*

21 *R. johnstoneanum*

22 *R. keysii*

23 *R. luteum*

24 *R. meddianum* var. *atrokermesinum*

25 *R. occidentale*

26 *R. orbiculare*

27 *R polyandrum*

28 *R. reticulatum*

29 *R. viscosum*

30 *R. wardii* var. *wardii* (Chamberlain)

31 *R. wardii* var. *wardii* (Chamberlain)

32 *R. xanthocodon*

33 *R. xanthocodon*

SPECIES FOR THE LARGE GARDEN
34 *R. arboreum*

35 *R. falconeri*

36 *R. fictolacteum*

37 *R. hodgsonii*

39 *R. lacteum*

38 *R. irroratum*

40 *R. macabeanum*

41 *R. ponticum*

42 R. planetum

44 R. rude

43 R. rex

45 R. uvariifolium

46 *R. vernicosum*

47 *R. vernicosum*

HYBRIDS FOR THE SMALL GARDEN
48 *R.* 'Elizabeth'

49 *R.* 'Elisabeth Hobbie'

50 *R.* 'Mucronatum'

51 *R.* × *praecox*

52 *R. × praecox*

53 *R.* 'Sylvester' (Kurume Azalea)

54 *R.* Vanessa 'Pastel'

55 *R.* 'Vuyks Scarlet' (Vuyk hybrid Azalea)

HYBRIDS FOR THE MEDIUM-SIZED AND LARGE GARDEN
56 *R.* 'Britannia'

57 *R.* 'Fire Glow' (Knaphill Azalea)

58 *R.* 'Christmas Cheer'

60 *R.* 'Cinnkeys'

59 *R.* 'Cinnkeys'

61 *R.* 'Crest'

62 *R*. 'Fusilier'

63 *R*. 'Ivanhoe'

64 *R.* 'Ken Burns'

65 *R.* 'White Cloud'

BARK EFFECT
66 *R. barbatum*

SPECTACULAR FOLIAGE
68 *R. sinogra:grande*

FOLIAGE EFFECT – AUTUMN COLOUR
67 *R. luteum*

GARDENS
69 Benmore Younger Botanic Gardens, Argyll

70 Crarae, Argyll

REGENERATION
71 Self-sown seedlings

grown. This is due principally to the difficulties in propagation and growing-on, resulting in a high price and low demand. For this reason, few species are normally offered for sale.

THE BOTANICAL GARDEN, NATIONAL TRUST AND SIMILAR BODIES

The botanical garden has several functions, among which is the provision of a wide range of uncommon plants. Due to their national and international standing, such gardens are frequently called upon to propagate, by various means, species which have been sent in by other botanical gardens or by plant collectors in the field. Because of the rarity value of these species, methods which are not commercially viable may be used to preserve, for example, the results of 6 months' trekking through the Himalayas.

In many countries, the existence of death duties, has led to large estates being handed over to the government. These are normally handed over, in turn, to non-profit making bodies, such as the National Trust, to be opened to the public for posterity.

These organisations are then put in a position similar to that of the botanical gardens, in that they have to maintain in perpetuity almost unique species. The biggest problem here is that they do not generally have sufficient money to carry out all the necessary work.

THE AMATEUR GROWER

The amateur growers are divided roughly into two main groups, those with a small town garden and those with a large suburban garden or small estate. The larger estates have invariably been forced to commercialise in order to offset the high running costs.

The facilities available to the amateur by way of propagation are generally limited by the need to supply only enough material for personal use and, perhaps, for that of a few friends. It is therefore unlikely that the amateur would wish to employ the sophisticated techniques of commercial growers but this should not alter the overall success rate.

The main difficulty faced by the amateur is the supply of correctly named stock plants as a source of cutting material. The best way round this problem is to become acquainted with some of the owners of the larger gardens who have inherited good collections and are willing to part with a few correctly taken cuttings. Alternatively, membership of the various societies which specialise in the genus enables contact with other enthusiasts and exchange of cutting material and seeds (see Appendix 6).

Propagation from Seed

One of the merits of the genus *Rhododendron* is the long flowering period (January to September in the northern hemisphere). This leads to an extended ripening period and consequently, to avoid premature dispersal of the seeds, several visits may be required to gather them.

The capsules, when mature, are usually dry, brown and curved, frequently with the remains of the style still attached. They are composed of a series of compartments, known as valves, containing the winged seeds. These become detached from the valve walls on maturity (Fig. 12).

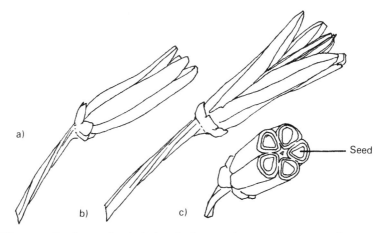

Seed

Fig. 12   Seed capsule: (a) closed, (b) opening, (c) in cross section.

It is not essential for the capsules to be totally dry, but they should have reached the stage where they break away freely under gentle pressure. The final drying stages can be completed in a warm dry room.

For information purposes, it is important that the parent plant is correctly labelled. Unfortunately, however, unless care is taken to ensure that open pollination does not occur, it is still quite likely that the resultant seedlings will contain a high proportion of hybrids. The likelihood of true offspring will be greatly increased if seed is collected from a plant in a garden where it is known that very few other species or hybrids are in flower at the same time. There is also always the possibility that another plant, quite unbeknown, may be in flower in the adjacent garden.

Equipment   The actual process of collection is quite simple; the only equipment required is some stout brown manila envelopes, a pencil, a small pair of secateurs or flower cutters, a clip-board for writing on and a receptacle, preferably waterproof, for the envelopes.

Labelling   An accurate record will prove invaluable in later years and, since the memory can prove to be only too fallible, it is vital that every possible detail is noted at the time of collection.

The initial information can be recorded either on the envelopes themselves or in a separate notebook, in which case each envelope must be numbered. The data to be recorded are as follows: date of collection, location, location within the garden — where appropriate, species or cultivar name, collector's number — if available, open or closed pollination. Write the information on the envelope before the seed is collected as this is extremely difficult to do when the envelope is full of capsules.

Gathering   The actual gathering of the seeds involves placing the envelope over the seed head and, with the secateurs, cutting the ripe truss from the plant. If the capsules have already started to split, extra care must be taken to ensure that the plant is disturbed as little as possible, to prevent the premature dispersal of the seed. In practice, the wind itself will disperse any seeds which are naturally ready for release. Remember to seal the mouth of each envelope carefully to prevent loss of seeds during transit.

Cleaning   Once the seeds are dry enough to fall freely away from the capsules, the cleaning process can take place. The simplest method is to shake out the seeds and debris on to a sheet of clean white paper. A gentle rubbing of the capsule between the fingers will ensure that any reluctant seeds are dislodged. A short length of stiff wire makes an ideal tool for separating the seeds and the larger pieces of chaff. If considerable quantities of seeds are to be dealt with, small wire sieves of various dimensions can be purchased to facilitate the process. If any difficulty is found in obtaining these sieves, a local botanical garden or agricultural college would almost certainly be able to recommend a supplier.

Although it is sometimes considered essential to ensure that the seeds are absolutely free of chaff, in order to avoid the onset of disease, in practice I have found that a small amount of debris makes very little difference, provided that the rest of the conditions are correct.

The clean seeds can be stored in small, dry, carefully labelled envelopes. It is important that the envelopes are dry because, if the gum is at all sticky, it becomes almost impossible to actually slip the seeds into the envelope. More importantly, damp conditions prior to sowing will reduce the period of viability.

Storage History records that various seeds, placed within the Pyramids by the ancient Egyptians, have germinated successfully more than 2000 years later. The main reasons for this incredible viability, are very low atmospheric humidity and freedom from fluctuating temperatures. The period of viability also depends on the species of seed. The modern technique of using foil packets to store flower and vegetable seeds relies on carefully controlled conditions at the time of packing, such as low moisture content and the almost total lack of air. With the correct environment, the rate of metabolism slows virtually to a standstill.

I am not aware that any rhododendron seeds are being offered to the public packed in this way at present. The temperature for storing seeds should not rise above 10°C or germination may be impaired.

SOWING THE SEED

Media A considerable amount of research has taken place to determine the ideal substrate, both for germinating and growing a wide range of flower and vegetable seeds.

The John Innes Research Institute pioneered the use of composts, manufactured to a very exacting standard, in a bid to reduce the vast numbers of individual composts used by the amateur and professional gardener. The basic constituents were loam, peat and sand, plus fertiliser and lime. The major drawback was the inevitable variability of the loam content.

More recently, soil-less composts marketed by several manufacturers have met with a great deal of success because the peat and sand, which are found in the majority, allow a uniformity which has hitherto been difficult to achieve. Rhododendrons, however, are seldom sown in this type of medium, principally because the commercially manufactured composts have a pH balance adjusted to suit a wide range of other genera. The high pH, which is normally calcium-based, will generally prove toxic to the seedlings of *Rhododendron.*

It is therefore necessary to find a substrate which will provide the ideal conditions for successful germination and seedling establishment. Without the correct levels of humidity, air and warmth, germination will be severely impaired.

It is important to remember that the type of substrate on which the seeds are sown should contain a constant balance of moisture and air (humidity), with only the temperature level being governed by the external conditions. Whatever medium is used, it must be free-draining, since waterlogging prevents oxygen reaching the seeds; on the other hand it should be able to hold sufficient moisture to allow a constantly humid atmosphere around the individual seed. Soil, when at saturation point, contains very little free oxygen, certainly insufficient for the germination of *Rhododendron* seed.

If *Rhododendron* seeds are allowed to fall to the ground, a small number will find the correct conditions for germination, but the proportion will be low compared with that which would be expected from manually sown seeds. Those seeds which have germinated will invariably be found growing in leafmould, peat or moss. From this natural selection, it can easily be deduced that at least one of these substrates should be suitable for the grower's needs. This has indeed proved to be true, for most people use and recommend either sphagnum moss alone or a combination of peat, leafmould and/or sphagnum. Sphagnum moss is particularly good, since it is impossible to overwater, provided that the surplus water can drain away freely.

I have successfully germinated seeds on a large piece of sphagnum placed in a pan, but it is difficult to prevent seeds falling down through the crevices in the moss. It is more practical to chop fresh sphagnum moss and mix it with fine leafmould in a proportion of 2:1. The leafmould should be from acid-based beech or oak, since any tree growing over an alkaline soil can produce high-pH-based leafmould which is totally unsuitable.

The combinations of sphagnum, peat and leafmould are endless and it is worth experimenting to determine which one suits your conditions. Once a good combination has been established it is advisable to continue using it for the more valuable species and perhaps to experiment with different mixtures for the less important varieties.

The medium should be placed in a 16-cm pan or similar container and filled to within 1 cm of the top. With a round piece of wood, or the base of another pan, as a tamping board, lightly press the surface until the level drops by about 2.5 cm. The containers are now ready for watering. They should be placed in a basin of water to approximately half their depth and left for a period of 12 hours or so, by which time the water will have entered through the drainage holes and thoroughly soaked the medium.

The containers should then be removed from the water and allowed to drain freely. The action of the water draining through will compact the medium to the correct degree of firmness. It will then be necessary to riddle a further quantity of medium to bring the level to within 2.5 cm of the top of the container. After about 3 hours, the newly riddled material will, by capillary attraction from the wet base, reach the correct moisture content for seed-sowing.

Temperature Once again there are differences of opinion as to the correct temperature for successful seed germination, but in my own experience a bottom heat of approximately 24.5°C will give an ideal temperature within the medium. It is advisable to allow about 12 hours for the filled pans to reach the optimum temperature.

Labelling It is vitally important that a proper system of identification be employed to ensure that the life history of the seeds can be charted. Probably the most commonly used label is the small plastic type which can be written on with a special pencil. Unfortunately this has not proved as permanent as some of the manufacturers claim; furthermore these plastic labels have a habit of becoming brittle with exposure to ultraviolet light.

The small metal labels are better for long-term use, although they do tend to corrode after a period of 3 to 4 years. It is interesting to note that the old-fashioned embossed lead labels can be found after 40 to 50 years, still clearly identifying many old plants in large, well-established gardens.

Some of the newer polycarbonate type of plastics may well prove to be a good source of permanent label material, since they are unbreakable and resistant to deterioration caused by ultra-violet light.

The information which should be recorded is similar to that required on the seed collecting envelopes, but with certain modifications. At this point it becomes essential to keep a diary or log of sowing data. On each label should be written the serial number to denote the batch of seed and the date of sowing, together with the source of the seeds and, most importantly, the species or hybrid name or parentage.

Sowing Seed sowing is in itself relatively simple, although care has to be taken to ensure that the density is correct. If you are in doubt, it is far better to err on the low side, for overcrowding will inevitably encourage the onset of damping-off disease.

Unless large quantities of seeds are being sown, I have found it quite practical to space-sow some of the seeds of the larger species since these are of a manageable size.

For the smaller species, a little dry silver sand mixed in with the seeds will allow you to spread them more evenly over the surface. Judging from the percentage germination, a sowing density of 57 to 100 per 16-cm pan, appears to be just about correct. If you take the trouble to count out the numbers of seeds, it can be seen just how inconsequential 100 seeds can look.

Germination   The containers should be placed in a propagating frame with a bottom heat of 24.5°C and covered with a sheet of glass and brown paper. Watering will not normally be necessary, providing germination takes place within 2 to 3 weeks, but occasionally batches of seed can take considerably longer, in which case a small hand-sprayer should be used to provide a fine misting of the surface.

Once germination has begun the paper should be removed, but care must be taken to avoid scorch from the direct rays of the sun. When approximately 25% of the estimated number of seeds have germinated the pans can be removed to a cooler temperature (around 15°C).

Aftercare   The natural process by which the root grows downward into the soil under the influence of gravity is called *positive geotropism*. The physiological term need not worry most growers, but the process is very noticeable in *Rhododendron* seedlings while they are still lying on the surface of the medium.

In practice a slightly better establishment after germination will be found if a very small amount of fine sterilised soil of low pH is riddled over the pans. This should be sufficient only to cover and anchor the young roots. This covering also helps to provide the minute amounts of nutrients which the seedlings will require before pricking out.

As the *Rhododendron* seedling does not respond too well to early handling, it is good practice to apply weak liquid feeding should there be any signs of mineral deficiency. There are many liquid feeds on the market, normally with a wide range of balanced elements to suit different crops at varying stages of growth. The general feed is quite suitable, but, as with any chemical, it is vital that the instructions be read carefully and it is a wise plan to halve the recommended dilution until experience has been gained.

The most commonly found complaint in seedlings is that of nitrogen deficiency but this can easily be cured by liquid feeding.

PRICKING OUT THE SEEDLINGS

If the seed has been sown in January or February, the seedlings should be ready for pricking out in June or July. Temptation to prick out earlier must be avoided since it is important that a good root system is established before moving the seedlings. If the seed has been sown at the correct spacing, the plants can easily be 2 cm high before it is necessary to move them on into large containers.

The seedlings should be pricked out to 2.5 cm apart, either into large seed pans or into plastic or wooden trays. No matter which type of container is used, it is essential that it should be perfectly clean to avoid the introduction of unwanted disease. The young seedlings are particularly susceptible at this stage.

It is important not to forget to label any extra containers used for the pricking out operation.

The young plants should be kept in a humid atmosphere at approximately 15°C for 1 week to allow them to establish themselves after the check. It is almost certain that the ambient temperature at the time of pricking out will be at least 15°C, in which case ventilation will be required.

Compost or Growing-On Medium The majority of enthusiasts make up their own compost. One which I have found suitable consists of: 1 part low-pH soil, preferably sterilised, passed through a 6 mm riddle; 1 part coarse quartz sand — alkaline shell sands are to be avoided; 1 part shredded sphagnum; 2 parts acid sphagnum peat; 1 part spruce or pine needles. All measurements are by volume. Other materials, such as leafmould or shredded tree bark, can be added or used as substitutes with equally good results.

The benefit of using soil in the compost is that normally there will be sufficient food within this loam to meet all the requirements of the seedlings during the establishment period.

Once the roots have started to grow into the new compost, the foliage should increase in size quite noticeably, but do not keep the temperatures too high (i.e. not above 10°C) in a bid to prolong active growth.

Overwintering There are two possible temperature regimes for overwintering the young *Rhododendron* plants.

If greenhouse space is available, the plants can be kept indoors, provided that continuous maximum ventilation is given at all times if the temperature rises above 5°C. The principal aim is to avoid forcing the plants into premature growth when the light levels are too low.

The other method of overwintering involves the use of north-facing frames outdoors. This low temperature regime uses no heat whatsoever and, because the sun cannot strike the frames, there should be no sudden heating and cooling of the plants.

If the overall temperature is kept low, by virtue of the external ambient conditions there should be no growth over the winter period. On the other hand, while one or two degrees of frost will cause very little harm, prolonged periods of frost with temperatures of −5°C or less will cause the compost to freeze solid; this is especially possible where the plants are in small containers above soil level. This is one good reason why it is beneficial to plunge the pans or trays into the soil within the frame. The framelights should be used to prevent waterlogging of the compost, although adequate ventilation must be given at all times, weather permitting.

Growing-On   In the spring, as the temperature begins to rise, the young plants will begin to show signs of growth. Initially, the apical buds will swell and, occasionally, some will open as flowers. This is only likely in the case of the small lepidote species, which naturally flower at an early stage of development. If this does occur, it is a good policy to remove the flowers carefully in order to prevent the plant concentrating its energy resources (which are severely limited at this age) on flowering. Once all danger of frost has passed, the framelight can be removed entirely and any plants which have died over the winter period should now be clearly distinguishable from the late starters. (This is especially relevant in the deciduous species.)

This is also a good time to check the plants for pests and diseases as the warmer weather brings out most of the insects and other pathogens from hibernation or overwintering stage.

TRANSPLANTING INTO POTS

Once the active growth has become apparent it will be necessary to space the plants out either into 75 mm pots or into specially prepared frames (Fig. 13).

Media   The compost used for pot work is similar to that for pricking out, but with the addition of a general balanced fertiliser. The quantity of fertiliser to be used will vary according to the unit value, which should be printed on the container in which it is packed.

The old and well tried John Innes Base Fertiliser is quite suitable at a rate of 3 g/l; it should, however, be noted that the limestone normally associated with standard composts must be omitted. The modern slow-release fertilisers can be used quite successfully when applied to the compost during the early part of the season. If used later, the nitrogen source will start to become effective when least desirable, that is, in the autumn, when the natural metabolism of the plant is slowing down. Careful handling of the plants is essential, if a severe check on growth is to be avoided. The plants should be lifted by the foliage only, after the roots have been teased loose from the original containers with a flat-pointed

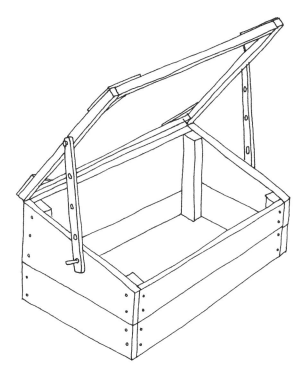

Fig. 13   Growing frame.

stick or small hand fork. Damage to the stem must be avoided since this will permit the entry of disease.

Potting   Standard potting techniques can be used but firming should be kept to a minimum and a good watering with a fine circular rose is all that is required to ensure the final settling of the compost around the roots. The pots should then be spaced out in a cool greenhouse with plenty of ventilation or placed outside in a frame or polyethylene tunnel. A light overhead spray with plain water will help to establish the plants, but it is essential to give adequate shading from the direct sun. When the roots have started to fill the container, repotting will be necessary and this must be carried out before the plants become potbound. It is undesirable to repot plants directly into containers more than two sizes larger than the original pot. This is because the soil tends to become stagnant and discourages further root development. The pots should never be allowed to dry out and an adequate water supply must be available at all times.

74

A good organic soluble fertiliser improves foliage colour and promotes vigorous growth. This may be applied during the early part of the summer, either by watering can or by spray-line if available. Feeding should be stopped when the first sign of firming up of the young growth is seen. A strict watch must be kept for pests and diseases and remedial measures taken if necessary.

DIRECT PLANTING INTO NURSERY BEDS OR FRAMES

I prefer the direct planting method because I believe that the plants are easier to look after, less susceptible to drying out and produce a better root system.

Construction of Nursery Beds   The use of old railway sleepers is a cheap but effective method of constructing nursery beds but, if these are not available, reclaimed timber can be used satisfactorily. The beds can be made up above ground level or a trench can be taken out and the sleepers laid out lengthwise to half their depth. The compost should consist of equal parts of good acid loam, partially rotted spruce or pine needles, peat and leafmould or crushed tree bark. In addition 3 kg of slow-release fertiliser should be applied per cubic metre.

The use of conifer needles in the compost promotes an extremely active root system which can almost be an embarrassment at lifting time. A strict watch has to be kept on the plants and a vertical cut with a spade will temporarily solve the problem of intertwining roots. I have grown many conifers as well as rhododendrons in this mix and found that large plants, which are normally difficult to transplant, can be moved at any time of the year without checking their growth. In Belgium, *R. simsii* hybrids are grown almost exclusively in a mixture containing a very high proportion of conifer needles.

Spacing   The distances at which the young plants should be set out will depend on the size of the species or cultivar grown. However, if you are prepared to move the larger species as soon as there is any sign of overcrowding, a uniform spacing can be used. Initially an interval of 10 cm, in rows 12.5 cm apart, will be satisfactory for the smaller species, while the larger ones are better spaced 15 cm by 20 cm respectively.

Labelling   Conventionally, the plants are labelled from the front to the back of the lines while working from left to right. As a double check, a plan showing the quantity and location of each species will be extremely helpful, especially where children and pets have access to your prized collection.

Watering and Feeding Provided that the plants are growing in a frame which is open to the weather, the amount of watering necessary will be considerably less than that required by most other methods. This will, of course, depend on the climate, but, with a rainfall of less than 100 cm spread throughout the year, a permanent irrigation system is a useful, if not essential, accessory. It should, however, be noted that the tender young leaves can be badly scorched if strong sunshine is allowed to fall on wet foliage.

If the plants are for any reason showing signs of a mineral deficiency an occasional liquid feed will usually restore their vigour.

Shading One benefit of modern technology is the wide range of available plastics which have found a use in horticulture.

A green polypropylene mesh, which is currently being used very successfully for cladding plastic tunnels, also provides both shade from strong sunlight and shelter from cold winds (Fig. 14). One major advantage of this mesh compared with standard polyethylene tunnels is in the provision of better ventilation in summer and lower humidity in winter.

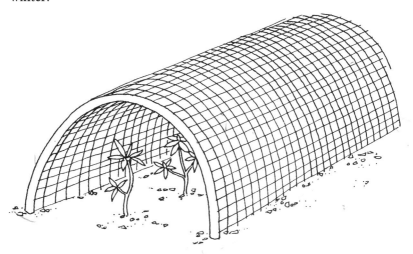

Fig. 14   Polypropylene mesh tunnel for shading.

The same material can be used to provide a temporary blind over the framelights during periods of strong sunshine. A framework will have to

76

be built around the outside of the frame to carry the material and it will then be a relatively simple matter to unroll the polypropylene as required. A secondary benefit of this type of construction is that it can be used to provide a measure of protection from late spring frosts.

Propagation from Cuttings

PRINCIPLES

Green plants, in order to grow, rely on the energy of the sun to convert carbon dioxide and water to usable starches and sugars. This process, known as *photosynthesis,* is dependent on the green pigment — chlorophyll.

A cutting, by its very nature, is incomplete. It lacks roots which, in the mature plant, normally supply water. The leaves, where photosynthesis mostly occurs, are necessary for growth but, at the same time, can lose valuable moisture to a dry atmosphere by means of transpiration and evaporation.

These problems must be overcome for successful propagation of cuttings. To ensure that the maximum amount of light reaches the leaf (with the exception of direct sunlight), the cuttings should be placed so that the laminae of the leaves are as nearly as possible at right-angles to the light source.

Cuttings will absorb a small amount of moisture through their cut stems and bases by osmosis but, providing the atmosphere is kept moist, by far the greatest amount will enter the stomata of the leaves (Fig. 15). A moist atmosphere can be achieved by constantly dampening the cuttings with a fine mist or by enclosing them in an impervious barrier, such as polyethylene film, to prevent natural humidity being lost (Fig. 16).

Most watering cans do not have a fine enough rose to dampen the leaf surface without saturating the rooting medium. It cannot be overemphasised just how important it is not to allow the rooting medium to become waterlogged. Lack of air at the base of the cutting will encourage the growth of various damping-off fungi and the eventual rotting of the cutting itself. However, a small hand-sprayer of the pump-action type is ideal for providing the mist-like conditions necessary and on a scale suitable for most amateurs and many professionals (Fig. 17).

If no protective film is used, it will be necessary to dampen the cutting at least six or seven times a day in cool conditions and even more when the weather is warm. This is an almost impossible task for the amateur

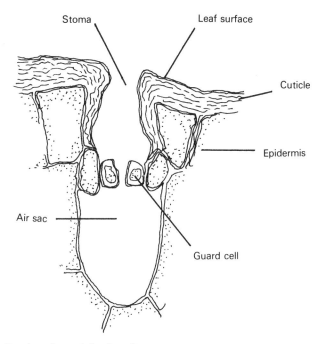

Fig. 15   *Section through leaf to show stoma.*

Fig. 16   *Propagation pit.*

78

Fig. 17   Spraying the cuttings.

without assistance. It is for this reason that some form of humidity control, such as the mist unit (p. 90) or framelight (p. 90) is recommended.

An hygrometer is a useful, although not essential, instrument. It can be purchased relatively cheaply from most garden centres or seedsmen and has a dial which indicates the relative humidity of the atmosphere. By ensuring that the reading never falls below 90% during the rooting operation, the percentage of successful cuttings will be greatly increased. It is probably true to say that most professionals seldom use this instrument but, for the beginner, it is a useful aid in a sometimes difficult situation.

Rooting can be further encouraged by the use of rooting hormones (p. 96) and by wounding to expose the cambium (p. 83).

SELECTION OF STOCK

The need to use clean, healthy and correctly labelled stock plants cannot be over-emphasised. When one considers the amount of work involved in nurturing cuttings through to flowering size, it would be foolish to end up with an incorrectly labelled, virus-infected plant, simply because of insufficient care at the propagation stage.

Identification The genus *Rhododendron* is notorious for the number of incorrectly labelled plants which are to be found, even in some of the most respected places. Nurserymen, not infrequently, offer plants which will never mature to resemble the specimens which you might have seen growing in a large collection. Even allowing for name changes and synonyms, there are still collector's numbers, clones and varieties, all of which add to the confusion.

If time and circumstance permit, it is a sensible precaution to visit, during the flowering season, the areas from where cuttings are to be taken to check the individual plants for features such as habit and flower colour and, if possible, to mark them with a label.

Stock Plants Professional nurserymen invariably have laid down what is known as a 'stock border'. The use of stock borders is perhaps more common in the case of those genera of shrubs with few species. In the genus *Rhododendron* there are probably about 600 species in cultivation and about 275 of these are offered by the larger nurseries. In addition, there are literally thousands of hybrids registered and several nurseries offer more than 100 of them.

The stock borders are therefore used only for the more common types, where it is feasible to set aside special plants to provide cuttings year after year and where the production of flowers is undesirable. They are not commonly used on large estates or in botanic gardens, where cutting material is taken from specimen plants growing *in situ*. The principal advantage of the stock border is in the provision of large quantities of young healthy cuttings from plants which have been specially groomed over many years. It also means that there is a greater chance that all plants offered for sale are true to type. These stock plants will have been given adequate quantities of fertiliser and pruned to produce the maximum quantity of young healthy non-flowering shoots.

Research has shown that, in the case of 'Exbury' hybrids, which can be difficult to overwinter, polyethylene covers over the stock plants will produce earlier cutting material. This enables the propagator to strike the cuttings earlier and thus have a better plant before the onset of cold weather.

COLLECTION OF CUTTING MATERIAL

The collection of cutting material should proceed along similar lines to that of seed collection. Propagation can usually be started in June (northern hemisphere) and continued through until October or November, according to the country, climate, season, latitude and species. The flowering time of the plants will certainly be an important feature, since young growth on the early-flowering species will ripen more quickly. As a general rule cuttings are taken when the wood is just beginning to ripen.

Equipment   The main requirements are a sharp knife or secateurs, a number of polyethylene bags, labels and a pencil.

There are many different opinions on what constitutes a perfect knife, but the one criterion with which the majority of propagators will agree is that it should have a good, well-balanced handle which can be easily held. The blade should be of high quality steel, capable of holding a razor-sharp edge for a reasonable period.

Sharpening a knife is a skill which can be acquired with practice. However, for those who prefer to use disposable blades, there are a number of good quality types which will prove ideal for the purpose. It is essential that the blade is kept sharp at all times for it can be a dangerous instrument when blunt. This might sound like a contradiction but, in fact, a blunt knife requires a lot more pressure to pull it through the wood and consequently is more difficult to control.

Selection of Cutting Material   It is best to take material from plants that are fully turgid. In the west of Scotland this is seldom, if ever, a problem but I have visited gardens in other parts of the country where the plants have been flagging so badly that any cutting material would have had only a marginal chance of survival. In such circumstances, it is highly desirable that the shrubs should be watered 2 to 3 days before cuttings are taken.

The ideal cutting should not contain an apical flowering bud. In practice this is often difficult to avoid, unless the stock plants have been specially prepared, and removal of these flower buds at preparation stage will be the only alternative. Thick, fleshy, long-jointed cuttings should be avoided if possible and so should underdeveloped hard woody specimens. The exception to this rule is the case of the deciduous azaleas in which cuttings should be struck from soft wood which has not had time to ripen.

The final length of the cutting will depend on the species concerned, but 10 cm is suitable for the larger species, while 4 cm will suffice for the smaller ones. In certain dwarf specimens, where very little young growth is being made, any cutting material longer than 2.5 cm will probably be difficult to find.

STORAGE OF CUTTING MATERIAL

Cuttings should preferably be prepared and inserted the same day as they are taken. If this is impossible, the cuttings can be stored in a cool damp atmosphere. They can be stored overnight in plastic bags inside a fridge at around 2°C — but they should not be put in the freezer compartment. It is interesting to note that, in the days of the early plant collectors, the only method of storage used was a metal case called a vasculum — a considerably heavier item than the polyethylene bag of today.

PREPARATION OF CUTTING MATERIAL

Trimming and Removal of Foliage   The trimming and removal of foliage is a subject open to argument. Some people contend that any damage to the foliage by way of trimming can pave the way for the onset of fungal disease. This may well be true to a certain extent, but when you consider that some species have foliage up to 0.9 m long then the difficulties of inserting them in a modest frame will be appreciated.

Where appropriate, to reduce moisture loss, the larger species should have their foliage trimmed to about half its length. Remember, however, that the survival of the cutting to rooting stage depends on the production of carbohydrates by photosynthesis — a process which occurs in the leaves. At the same time, a few of the lower leaves, which would obviously be below the level of the rooting media, can be removed. A balance between photosynthesis and moisture loss is the aim.

Types of Cuttings   There are four basic types of standard semi-hardwood cuttings: the standard nodal, internodal and single and double wounding. The last of these is the most popular for the medium-sized species and cultivars.

The standard nodal cutting is probably the most common method of plant propagation. A clean cut should be made just below the node, at right-angles to the stem. It is generally recognised that the bulk of the rooting hormones occur in this region. There are two ways in which the cut can be made, either towards the body, with the thumb being used as an anvil, or downwards on to a soft piece of wood or rubber.

Most experienced propagators use the former method unless the cuttings are particularly hard. Note that it is not difficult to take small slices out of the thumb at the same time! A home-made rubber thimble is a useful gadget which is often employed where large numbers of semi-hardwood cuttings are being taken.

Internodal cuttings, where the cut is made midway between the nodes, have been used with much success in those genera with many climbing shrubs, such as *Vitis* and *Clematis*. This method has been tried on Kurume azaleas with mixed results. The Kurumes are generally short-jointed and it is relatively difficult in many cases to take anything else but internodal cuttings.

The wounding technique, both single and double, is now being applied widely to a large range of medium-sized shrubs, including *Rhododendron*. Although experiments are continuing with this method, results so far look extremely promising. A cut approximately 2.5 cm long should be made in a downwards direction on one or both sides of the cutting (Fig. 18). This increases the area of cambium exposed (the area of actively dividing cells where the root initials are formed) and is believed to give the cutting a better chance of rooting.

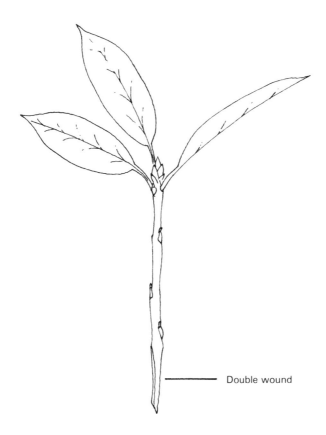

Double wound

Fig. 18   Nodal cutting showing double wound.

Kinsealy Research Station has reported that the percentage of cuttings rooted by single or double wounding is about the same. Although the single wound does produce a slightly unbalanced root system to start with, this does not affect the plant materially.

The length of cut will depend on the species concerned and, in the really dwarf types, no wounding should be used.

INSERTION OF CUTTINGS INTO MEDIUM

Details of media suitable for rooting cuttings are given on p. 94. The use of a dibber to make a small hole in the medium for cutting insertion has for a long time been a universally accepted practice but today, if the cuttings are sufficiently firm, the general trend is to use the stem itself to make the hole. The cuttings are then inserted in the medium to approximately half their length, although this varies from species to species.

TRANSPLANTING AND POTTING-ON

The length of the rooting period varies according to species and cultivar. Bearing this in mind, it is extremely unlikely that all cuttings in one section of a frame will root at the same time and therefore some will have to be removed before others.

The main criterion for removal is the formation of an adequate root system, capable of supporting the plant in a less favourable environment. Within the frame there is a warm humid atmosphere, while, outside, the plant will be subjected to fluctuating temperature and a much lower humidity. It is therefore desirable to try to establish the root system within the compost before too violent a change takes place.

The rooted cuttings should be carefully lifted by inserting a small flat piece of wood or plastic below the level of the roots and gently teasing upwards. Any cuttings which have not rooted sufficiently can be returned to the rooting medium for a further week or two. Make sure that the remaining cuttings are still labelled. The compost used should be identical to that recommended for the transplanting of seedlings into pots.

The size of pots will depend on the size of the species or cultivar involved. The small types will be quite happy in 5 cm diameter pots, while the larger species will require pots of 8 cm diameter.

Firming of the compost must be kept to a minimum; watering the potted cuttings will usually firm the compost sufficiently. The pots

Fig. 19   Lifting a rooted cutting of R. burmanicum *after 8 weeks.*

should then be returned to the frame for a period of 7 to 10 days to encourage the young root system to move into the new medium. If the shortage of room does not permit this, the plants should be given a fine overhead misting with a small hand-sprayer at least twice a day for a week. The potting dates should be recorded in a register.

FURTHER MANAGEMENT

The further management of rooted and potted cuttings is identical to that described for seedlings at a similar stage of development. It is a matter of choice whether the young plants are planted directly into frames or potted on into larger containers.

HEALTH AND HYGIENE

One of the first principles in horticulture is the maintenance of a clean and disease-free environment. This is impossible to achieve unless the cuttings themselves are in good condition when they are taken from the plant. Certain pests and diseases may be relatively innocuous outdoors under cool and dry conditions. However, once the host plants are exposed to a vastly more favourable environment, multiplication and spread of

85

disease organisms can reach epidemic proportions. Rhododendrons as a genus are relatively free of the serious problems to which more intensely cultivated crops, such as chrysanthemums, are prone, but vigilance must be kept.

Rejection of poor quality or damaged cuttings is the first step in good plant husbandry. With experience and knowledge of the genus the more difficult-to-root species will be quickly recognised and even greater care should then be taken with their day-to-day management. Removal of any leaves or cuttings which have died will help to prevent the build-up of fungal pathogens.

Certain professional growers change the rooting medium after each batch of cuttings, but in practice, providing that there is no known pest or disease problem endemic to the medium, the removal of the used material once every 6 to 9 months will be sufficient. Local authorities tend to reduce the operation to once per year and generally carry this out in the winter, when the greenhouse units are being washed down. I have known parks departments to have left the same medium in their propagating benches for 2 or even 3 years without any serious ill-effects, although this is not recommended.

In hard-water areas, rainwater should be used to avoid the build-up of calcium and other salt deposits on the foliage. It is advisable to maintain a tank of water in the greenhouse or porch where it can warm up before being used.

As with many other genera, *Rhododendron* contains species and cultivars which vary greatly in their ease of rooting. It should therefore be remembered that even the experts who have been working with the genus for many years still have their failures and experiments are continuing to try to improve the percentage of rooting.

Cuttings may be propagated either indoors in greenhouses or outdoors in frames. The former method is probably the most common although there are advantages in both.

Equipment and Materials for Indoor Propagation

PROPAGATION BENCH

The construction of a propagation bench has not changed much in the last 30 years, although modern materials have enabled the design to be adapted to produce a lighter more portable bench, which even the non-skilled can build. A typical design is shown in Fig. 20 and this can be adapted to suit requirements.

Fig. 20   Propagation bench.

The slotted angle should preferably be galvanised, although I have used standard finished material in a porch, where the corrosion element is less than that of a greenhouse. The slotted angle can be purchased pre-cut to size or a hacksaw can be used to cut the full lengths, which are normally 3 m long.

The base and sides should be of 22 m exterior quality plywood which has had two applications of non-toxic wood preservative about 1 week before use. Holes 7.5 mm in diameter and 30 cm apart should be drilled in the base to allow the free drainage of surplus water. If the bench is going to be housed in a porch or similar structure, the drainage holes should be omitted and the entire inside of the unit lined with 500 gauge polyethylene sheeting. In this instance, extra care must be taken to prevent waterlogging. The bottom of the bench is then covered with 5 cm of coarse, washed, river or quarried sand (shell sand must not be used).

It is generally accepted that the provision of bottom heat greatly facilitates the rooting of most species of *Rhododendron,* although it must be pointed out that several species, principally *R. simsii* hybrids, will root quite happily without it. Other species will take much longer and the percentage rooting will be lower.

In the British Isles, the number of commercial establishments using electrical space heating on a large scale is practically nil. On the other hand, electric heaters are relatively common among amateur growers, principally because, although the running costs are high, the simplicity, cost of installation and the ease of maintenance are normally lower than with any other system. Electricity is also very simple to control and there is an extensive range of sophisticated equipment available.

Electricity comes into its own particularly in the provision of bottom heat for propagation. This does not mean that hot water pipes, heated by gas, oil or solid fuel cannot be used, but they are more difficult to install and to control on a small scale.

Soil-Heating Cables Soil-heating cables are probably the ideal method, since any shape of propagating bench can be accommodated easily.

As with any item of electrical equipment, it is important that both the manufacturer's instructions and the supply board's regulations are closely followed, since there is always an element of danger, especially under the wet conditions in which the cables will be used. If you are in any doubt about your ability to install the equipment, a local, reputable electrical contractor should be contacted. Electrical voltage varies from country to country and calculations must be made before purchasing the correct length of cable. Table 3 gives an approximate guide to the length of cable required, although the manufacturer's data sheet should be consulted before purchase.

Table 3 Length of cable required to heat a given area of propagating bench (at 220/240 volts AC/DC).

Watts	Length of cable (m)	Area covered (m²) Standard bench	Mist bench
75	6	1	0.5
150	12.25	2	1
300	24.5	3.75	2
500	40.5	6	3.75

The heating cable should be spaced out along the length of the bench on the surface of the sand so that there is an even space between each run of cable. Small pieces of wire can be used to hold the cable in position while the spacing-out operation continues and these should be removed on completion of the work. If the heating cable is being laid while ambient temperatures are low, flexibility can be improved by switching on the current for 10 minutes before commencing the work.

A further 5 cm of sand is laid on top of the cable and smoothed level with a board. A hole should be drilled through the side to take the thermostat, which should then be installed with the rod resting just below the surface of the sand. A further 5 cm of rooting medium is then placed over the sand and levelled with a board. The thermostat and the heater are now ready to be wired together as described in the manufacturer's instructions.

Thermostatic Control   The use of a reliable thermostat not only makes the system of control simple and accurate but also reduces the running cost.

There are many makes of thermostat available but the most suitable consists of a tube of brass or other non-corrosive metal, containing the heat sensor. This is fixed to a plastic or metal alloy box, which houses the electrical control gear. It is essential not to use an ordinary house-type thermostat as these are not normally designed to withstand the corrosive conditions encountered during propagation.

PROTECTION OF CUTTINGS

Cladding   The use of glass frames as an aid to propagation has been with us for at least 100 years and is still popular today. Plastics, however, are now making considerable inroads and many growers have changed to polyethylene covers. Either may be used for cladding the framelight.

Glass can be purchased already cut to size although it is a relatively simple job to cut the sheet to the right size using a glass cutter. Horticultural glass is most commonly sold by weight, either 24 or 32 oz. With the advent of metrication, the thickness 3 or 4 mm is becoming the criterion for measurement.

Polyethylene can be purchased in rolls of varying widths and thicknesses, which are measured in gauge size or μ unit. An ultra-violet inhibitor is usually added to prevent discoloration by sunlight.

Polyethylene is not only cheaper than glass but is also lighter and unbreakable. The light transmission quality, while not quite as good as glass, is adequate for propagation purposes. White polythene has a certain advantage over its clear counterpart in the management of the cuttings as certain species of deciduous azaleas are readily scorched by sun and, unless particular care is taken, the foliage can be irreparably damaged. However, this advantage is largely lost where the frame faces north and receives only the very early winter sun.

Framelight Structure The structure of the framelight depends on the material used for cladding. Glass cladding requires a well-jointed, treated wood or aluminium alloy frame. Although the aluminium alloy frame will probably cost more initially, the ease of maintenance and cleaning, together with better light reflection, will be advantageous. Wood, on the other hand, is cheap and, provided it has been treated well in advance with a non-toxic wood preservative, the life-span should be long enough for most grower's needs.

Wood is slightly easier to work with than aluminium alloy if polyethylene film is to be used for cladding. 200 gauge polyethylene sheeting can be fixed to the frame by tacking it to a wooden baton 6 mm thick, which is then nailed to the top of the frame. The sheeting is pulled tight to the opposite end where it is fixed with another baton.

Polyethylene of between 80 and 100 gauge is now being used very effectively as a cheap and simple alternative to mist propagation, although unfortunately, it is not always easy to obtain the correct gauge of polyethylene. In this case, after the cuttings have been inserted in the bench, the polyethylene film is stretched over them and sealed at the edges.

Research has shown that the percentage of cuttings rooted by this method is almost as high and, in certain species, higher, than the percentage achieved under mist.

MIST-TYPE PROPAGATION BENCH

The mist bench is virtually identical in construction to the non-mist type except that there are no elevated sides.

The cable loading should be 75 watts per square metre (see Table 3). Good drainage is important since the rooting medium can easily become waterlogged if there is a malfunction in the misting gear control.

MIST SYSTEM

There are several items of relatively simple equipment which are totally dependent on one another for the successful functioning of the bench. The recommended operating pressure is 3–4 kg/cm^2 but satisfactory performances can be achieved at slightly lower pressures.

Atomiser Jets   There are several manufacturers producing atomiser jets (Fig. 21) which all work on similar principles. The jets are usually constructed of a non-corrosive metal, such as brass or stainless steel, although plastic is being used by some companies. A fine mesh filter is often incorporated to trap particles of dirt in the water supply and thus prevent the jets from becoming blocked.

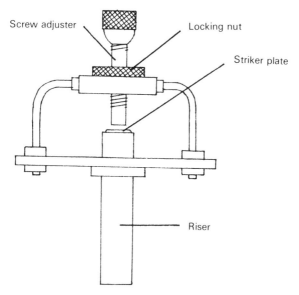

Fig. 21   Misting head.

The mist effect is formed when the water, which leaves the jet at a great velocity, hits the striker plate and is broken up into fine droplets. The spacing of the jets is normally at 1 m intervals.

The following table can be used as a guide for the calculation of jet size, although the manufacturer's data should be checked before any purchase is made.

Table 4   Calculation of jet size.

Jet size	Maximum bench width (m)	Discharge per jet (l/hr)
1	1.05	16
2	1.20	27
3	1.35	36

The Plumbing of a Mist System   As mentioned earlier, consultation with a local water authority is advisable. Most publish sets of regulations which are easily followed and, if there should be difficulties, they are quite willing to explain any relevant point.

It is essential to incorporate gate valves wherever possible so that parts of the system can be isolated for repairs and the water supply can be closed down completely whenever necessary. Compression joints are preferable to capillary types since they are much easier to alter should the system be developed in future years. High pressure polyethylene piping is now permitted for cold water supply by most water authorities and this is less vulnerable to frost should the heating system break down.

The water supply is normally fed through plastic pipes buried within the bench, although, quite frequently, overhead pipes are used. Those pipes which are buried have a riser fitted at 1 m intervals, while the overhead piping has the atomiser jets screwed directly into the main feed pipe. The solenoid valve is the centre of the control system and is operated electronically from the control unit. An in-line filter is frequently fitted in the water supply system before the solenoid valve. The mesh screen prevents dirt which could eventually cause a blockage reaching the solenoid valve. Where the water pressure is below 3–4 kg/cm^2, it is recommended that a pressure pump be fitted to the system. There are several types available which are activated either directly, by a relay in the control box, or indirectly, by feeding a pressure tank or similar device.

If you are in any doubt about the existing pressure it is advisable to consult the water board as these pumps can be fairly expensive to buy and occasionally require servicing. It may well be possible for the water board to supply you with a new pipe which would increase the available pressure for about the same price as a pump, and thereafter the system would be cheaper to operate. In any case it is advisable to check with the local authority in case there are any regulations which have to be met. These can vary from region to region and from country to country, so it is impossible to list any hard and fast rules.

Water Flow Regulators   The flow of water to the misting or atomiser jets must be regulated and there are three systems in common use: the electronic leaf, the timer unit and the solar control unit. The choice of system will be related to personal circumstances and preferences. If possible, growers should be visited who use the systems, so that their operation can be checked before a final decision is made.

The electronic leaf has been, and probably will remain, the most common system of control, although the other two methods are gaining favour. It consists of two conducting electrodes set in a bakelite or other plastic matrix. These are fixed on a rod and are connected by cable to the main control unit. The electronic leaf is positioned among the cuttings on the bench and it works on the assumption that the rate of evaporation from the leaf is the same as that from the cuttings. When the atomiser jets operate, a fine film of moisture bridges the gap between the electrodes, thus completing a circuit which de-energises the solenoid valve, thus stopping the jets. As the moisture evaporates, the circuit is broken, the solenoid is energised and the atomiser jets are activated again.

There are advantages and disadvantages in this system. Poor positioning of the leaf materially affects the evaporation rate and the surface of the sensor can become covered either in salt deposits, which will permanently complete the circuit, or grease, which can keep the circuit constantly open. Cleaning the surface with methylated spirits or a similar substance invariably cures the problem. However, in climates where the weather is so variable that considerable temperature fluctuations are experienced in a short period of time, thus leading to rapid changes in the evaporation rate, this system is ideal and, assuming that it is functioning perfectly, it is possibly the best for northern climates.

The timer unit operates by switching the current to the solenoid on and off at pre-set but variable intervals. It in no way takes into account the evaporation rate and has to be set manually, according to the weather. It can be purchased as an independent unit or as part of a weaner unit. Its main advantage to the professional is its reliability. Also it suffers from none of the problems which sometimes beset the electronic leaf. Since the professional nurseryman is usually working close to the propagation unit, the setting can be quickly and easily varied according to the weather. This is not usually possible for the amateur, who is normally working during the day. However, where the temperatures are expected to be constant throughout the day, the system can be used by the amateur with great success. The principal danger is that a sudden drop in the evaporation rate will lead to surplus water running off the leaves and waterlogging the rooting media.

The third system is the solar control unit. The principle by which this operates is not new, in as much as the use of photoelectric cells has been common practice in other fields for many years. It has, however, only recently been developed successfully for mist propagation and is still to be adopted extensively by professional growers. The frequency of the misting is dependent on the prevailing light conditions and is variable from about every 1½ minutes on a bright day to 20 minutes or more during dull weather. There is also a facility for a short burst of mist at night when evaporation is taking place.

Hard-Water Areas While steps can be taken to rectify soil conditions for the successful cultivation of the genus in high-pH areas, propagation using hard-water can present difficulties on two accounts: furring up of misting jets and ancillary equipment, and deposits on the foliage and in the rooting media, leading to the eventual death of the cutting. Various softening units are available which overcome this problem by the chemical process known as cation exchange.

Weaner Unit The weaner unit is used to gradually acclimatise rooted cuttings to the slightly harder, and therefore less favourable, conditions experienced in the natural environment. Controlled by manual pre-setting, the weaner unit operates by reducing the frequency of misting until it can be dispensed with entirely. A separate bench is useful, although not essential, for the best results.

Rooting Media

There are a number of different media in use, all having one feature in common, namely a facility for good drainage combined with the ability to retain the correct amount of moisture. This is normally achieved by the particle size being as uniform as possible. Many other media are undergoing trials at the moment, but the results are as yet unavailable or inconclusive due to insufficient data.

There are no hard and fast rules about which medium to choose; each has its merits and demerits depending on the locality, conditions and culture. Research units throughout the world have carried out experiments to find the ideal medium and each one has come forward with different but equally valid results. You are advised to try a few of the media described below until a suitable one is found.

PEAT

There are many different brands of peat on the market but there are only two basic types: the sedge peats, derived principally from the genus *Carex,* and the sphagnum peats from the many species of the moss genus *Sphagnum.*

For our purposes, only the best quality of sphagnum should be used.

This is the younger peat, which has been extracted from near the top of the bog and it should contain visible and identifiable remnants of the parent plant. Because of its large particle size, this type of peat contains more air spaces, which are essential for good drainage.

For many years, the Kinsealy Research Centre in Dublin has carried out experiments on the propagation of rhododendrons using pure sphagnum peat as a rooting medium. They introduced various other factors, such as different fertilisers, timing, wounding, but each one depended on pure peat as a substrate. Successful results proved that peat by itself is a very adequate medium for both beginner and expert alike.

It should, of course, be emphasised that the quality of the peat, and the overall care with which the cuttings are treated, play a vital role in the success rate.

SAND

There are many types of sand available but very few are of a quality suitable for use as a rooting medium. Ideally the particle size, as mentioned earlier, should be uniform, to provide optimum drainage. The best sands are sometimes given a number according to the type and particle diameter, which in this case should be about 3 mm.

Sand by itself has been used for many years, especially in the case of those plants which tend to rot off quickly at the base, and it can be especially useful for the large-leaved species which take longer to root. Sand is a very heavy material and, when used alone, extra support for the propagating bench is often required.

PEAT AND SAND

A 1:1 mixture of peat and sand of the same qualities described above is frequently used as a medium. It provides an ideal balance between moisture retention and drainage and is certainly to be recommended for most species.

PERLITE

Perlite is an expanded volcanic rock, white in colour, very light in weight and with a diameter of approximately 4 mm. It is available in different size packs. It can be dusty and quite a problem should a bag accidentally burst inside a vehicle.

Perlite and peat as a rooting medium is gaining favour amongst propagators of a wide range of shrubs, including rhododendrons. The ratios vary but both 1:1 and 1:3 have given good results. A high quality peat must be used to provide good water retention combined with plenty of air spaces.

VERMICULITE

This is an expanded form of mica rock which has been used extensively for seed germination, but it is reported to be too moisture-retentive for satisfactory results with rhododendrons.

CRUSHED TREE BARK

Crushed tree bark is the semi-decomposed waste from conifers which have been debarked prior to use by the sawmills. It has been used widely as a mulch but there is little information available at present on its suitability as a rooting medium for rhododendrons, although trials with other genera indicate that it may prove to be as good as peat.

A mixture of tree bark and pumice in a ratio of 3:1 is being used in New Zealand.

Rooting Hormones

The use of rooting hormones in both the amateur and professional fields has been fairly common practice for about 25 years. The three most commonly used are indolebutyric acid (IBA), indoleacetic acid and naphylacetic acid.

These hormones are usually available in different formulations and there is considerable controversy over which hormone or formulation produces the best results. To further complicate matters, experiments made with different strengths (as denoted by % active ingredient) have produced varying results, according to the rhododendron species or cultivar on trial.

Kinsealy Research Centre have carried out many experiments to determine the ideal formulation, type etc. and have consistently settled for 0.8% IBA as a control.

In 1969, trials were carried out to investigate the effects of various % IBA powders, plus 5% captan dust, and a 4000 p.p.m. solution quick-dip treatment. The hybrid used was 'Britannia', which is difficult to root. On this occasion the quick-dip method was found to be the most successful, giving 42% rooting after 10 weeks.

However, in the following year, the results from the quick-dip method were actually poorer than when the 0.8% powder was used the previous year. This may have been due to several factors, such as turgidity of the cuttings, ripeness of the wood, a slight difference in season.

In 1971, trials continued with three cultivars as shown in Table 5.

Table 5   Effect of growth hormone on percentage rooting.

| Cultivar | Percentage rooting | |
	IBA 0.8%	No hormone
'Purple Splendour'	78	18
'Britannia'	12	2
'Pink Pearl'	56	36

The above experiment was carried out both under plastic sheeting and mist, each method giving results in a similar proportion.

Further trials continued in subsequent years and, in the case of deciduous azalea cultivars, such as 'Gold Dust' and 'Ballerina', it was shown fairly conclusively that, while the powder did not increase the speed of rooting, the actual percentage rooted was considerably greater.

It has been common practice in the past for the powders to be supplied in three different strengths, according to the age of the wood on which they are to be used. One manufacturer has now produced a single powder which, it is claimed, will be suitable for a wide range of cutting material. The main benefit of the powder formulation to the amateur, and often the professional, is the longer storage life and the ease of use.

Layering

Layering can be regarded, in many ways, as a form of insurance. The principle, as with ordinary cuttings, relies on the plant's natural ability to produce roots from stems. The two forms of layering frequently used in the propagation of new plants are in no way restricted to the genus *Rhododendron*.

GROUND LAYERING

Certain species of plants, notably the ivies and other true climbers, produce what are known as *adventitious roots* along their stems. By means of these, the plants gain support from walls, trees, etc. and also they can be propagated easily by the removal and pegging down of the rooted sections. At a later date, the stem, which acts as an 'umbilical cord', can be severed and the young plant should then be capable of leading an independent existence.

Within the *Rhododendron* group, there are species, such as *R. forrestii repens,* whose creeping habit encourages the natural production of rooted layers. However, the majority of species have an upright or semi-upright form of growth and these will require assistance.

Preparation of the Ground As for the propagation of cuttings, a suitable rooting medium is required. With few exceptions, the soil surrounding semi-mature plants is unsuitable for the successful layering of branches without the incorporation of peat and sand or similar material.

A shallow trench should be taken out around the base of the parent plant, but great care must be taken not to damage the root system. The soil removed should then be mixed with sufficient of the chosen medium to give good moisture retention as well as good drainage. Experience is the best guide to the amount of medium as variability of soil types makes it difficult to quantify. The trench should then be backfilled with the mixture and lightly tramped to consolidate the soil.

Layering into containers is often employed successfully in preference to the trench method as this reduces the check on growth caused by the lifting operation.

Method The best material for layering is usually found on branches which are too far from the ground to be of service to the propagator. The ideal subject is a shoot, 1 or 2 years old and near enough to the base of the plant to be bent down to ground level.

Several different methods are used for inducing root production. The one often advocated is to make an oblique incision on the underside of the stem to approximately one-third of its diameter; into this insert a small piece of wood to keep the cut open and then bend the shoot at right-angles, at which point it can be pegged down into the soil. Hormone rooting powder can be added to the cut surface as well but I have seen no controlled experiments to prove that this is in any way advantageous. Certain growers merely twist the stems to check the sap flow and then bend the branch at right-angles.

Removal and Transplanting The time taken to form a root system large enough to support an independent plant will vary according to species but it is often in the region of 18 months. Unless there is a specific

98

reason for its early removal, it is advantageous to leave the young plant *in situ* for a month or two after severing it from the parent plant, to ensure that the root system is well established. Once the plant has been lifted, aftercare is similar to that described for seedlings.

AERIAL LAYERING

Aerial layering as a means of propagation is used quite widely on many species, including indoor plants such as *Ficus elastica*.

On rhododendrons it is generally carried out where it is impossible to propagate the plant by the more common method of ground layering. Any person who has visited, for the first time, a large garden where this method is being extensively employed, may well be surprised to find what looks like polyethylene bags fixed to the branches! Aerial layering can take place at any time of the year provided that a length of mature stem is available.

Method The selected branch is bent downwards, so that the apex is towards the propagator, and, with a sharp knife, an oblique cut is made, approximately one-third to half the stem diameter, on the top of the stem in the direction of the growing tip. The cut is then held open with a small twig or piece of plastic (Fig. 22a). The use of hormone rooting powder is once again optional.

A large wad of sphagnum moss, from which all surplus moisture has been squeezed, is then placed around the stem so that the cut surface is completely covered. A length of polyethylene, 15–20 cm wide, is then wrapped tightly around the sphagnum and sealed with waterproof adhesive tape (Fig. 22b). There is some controversy over whether the bottom as well as the top of the polyethylene should be sealed, as it has been shown that excessive moisture retained in the sphagnum will lead to a poor success rate. Therefore, if you cannot be certain of preventing rain entering the sphagnum from the top, it is wise to leave the lower aperture slightly open to allow for drainage. On the other hand, by sealing both ends, a uniform moisture content can almost certainly be guaranteed, provided that no rain can enter.

It is worth noting that polyethylene film is available in a tubular form which many people find easier to use.

Removal and Transplanting A root system sufficiently large to support independent growth should be visible after 12 to 18 months (Fig. 22c); if this is not the case the layer should be left for a further 6 to 12 months, by which time, barring unforeseen problems, success will have been achieved.

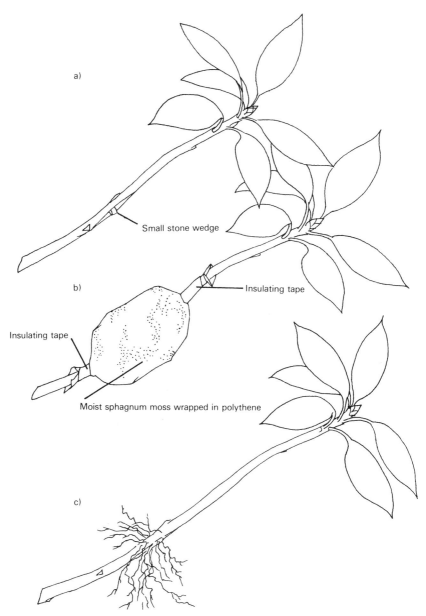

a)

Small stone wedge

b)

Insulating tape

Insulating tape

Moist sphagnum moss wrapped in polythene

c)

Fig. 22 *Aerial layering: (a) slit stem, (b) stem bound with moss, (c) new root formation.*

The layer should be cut from the parent with a pair of sharp secateurs, just below the joint at which the roots have formed. The polyethylene must be removed carefully to leave the sphagnum intact. Difficulty is often experienced at this point of transition between an aerial root system and a totally independent soil system. The roots will almost certainly be very soft and somewhat lacking in the harder fibrous tissue normally found on those plants which have been growing in the soil. A good open mix, as described in the section on transplanting seedlings, must be used for potting.

Grafting

Grafting has been used extensively in the past for the rapid production of young fruit trees, tailor-made for specific purposes. Research units developed special root stocks which would produce plants ideal in habit for situations as varied, for example, as small gardens, large orchards and areas of heavy soil.

In the genus *Rhododendron*, grafting was used chiefly to provide plants of cultivars which had proved difficult to root by normal methods. However, grafting has declined in popularity, due principally to the improvements in rooting techniques. The main disadvantage in grafting is the frequent appearance of suckers, which, if left unchecked, soon take over the main cultivar. Many neglected gardens are now derelict, having been overgrown by *R. ponticum,* the parent root stock of most of the fine old hybrids.

PRINCIPLES

Many examples of natural grafting can be seen in deciduous forests, where one branch has rubbed against another and eventually stayed in close enough contact, and for long enough, for the two branches to unite. The areas which join are just below the surface of the bark and are composed of actively dividing cells which make up the cambium. Callus formation in the area of the join subsequently binds together the two components.

Several types of grafting are practised, each depending on two essential parts: the *root stock* and the *scion*. The root stock, as the name implies, is the plant which provides the rooting system for the cultivar or species which is to be propagated. The species most commonly used for this is probably *R. ponticum,* although work is also being done on others, such as

R. decorum and the cultivar 'Cunninghams White'. The scion is the cultivar or species to be propagated. Thus the strong rooting qualities and strong main stem of the root stock are combined with the good flowering qualities of the scion.

Any grafting operation must be carried out with almost surgical precision and the two cut surfaces must be held as close together as possible to assist callousing and unification. As with fruit trees, occasional difficulties may be experienced in getting the scion to 'take' on the root stock.

COLLECTION AND SELECTION OF THE ROOT STOCK

The root stock can be grown either from cuttings or from seed in the normal way or from seedlings collected in the wilds of an estate (providing permission has been obtained, of course). The ideal plant will have a stem about the thickness of a pencil and will be free of pests and diseases.

The scion wood should be identical in diameter to the root stock and, likewise, free of pests and diseases. It is worth checking the validity of the name, for, as with cuttings, a lot of effort will be wasted if the parent plant turns out to be incorrectly labelled. If several different cultivars are being grafted at the same time, tie-on paper labels should be fixed to each individual scion at the time of collection.

PREPARATION OF THE ROOT STOCK

The young root stocks should be potted into 9-cm pots approximately 4 to 6 weeks before the proposed date of grafting. These root stocks can then be transferred to a greenhouse or heated frame, kept at a temperature of approximately 15°C and frequently syringed. Within a few weeks, new roots will form and the foliage will show signs of growth.

Equipment A razor-sharp knife is vital for success. Polyethylene strips approximately 2.5 cm wide, which can be purchased in rolls specifically for grafting and budding, or the more traditional materials, such as rubber or raffia, will also be required. A grafting case, although useful, is not essential. This can be built in the same way as the propagation bench described earlier, but with the addition of elevated sides and a framework to take the polyethylene sheets.

METHODS OF GRAFTING

There are several methods of grafting in current use: the modified side graft, the veneer graft and the saddle graft. None is unique to the genus *Rhododendron*, although saddle grafting is commonly associated with it. Saddle grafting can be carried out during the late winter or early spring, although there is no reason why it should not be successful at other times. The main advantage of early grafting is that the work can take place in a greenhouse or potting shed where there is less pressure on time and room. There is also less likelihood of high temperatures which might lead to wilting of the scion before union is achieved.

Saddle Grafting   Like many other specialised procedures in horticulture, this is relatively simple to carry out after the initial skill has been obtained. It is therefore worth practising on extra or unnamed material before working on the species or cultivar to be propagated.

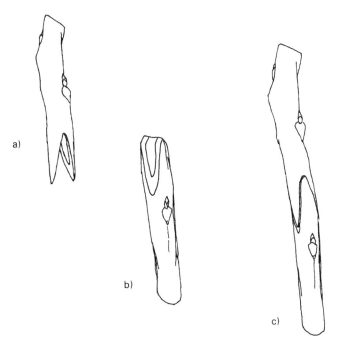

Fig. 23   Saddle grafting: (a) scion, (b) stock, (c) saddle graft.

Two cuts, about 18 mm long and slanting inwards to form a V shape, should be made in the base of the scion. A sharp turn of the knife at the end of each cut will form a kind of saddle. The root stock is cut in a similar way, as closely to the base as possible, to take the saddle. Match the cuts as closely as possible and join the two parts together. If this part of the operation has been carried out correctly it will be possible to turn the whole plant upside down without the scion falling out. The junction of root stock and scion should then be firmly bound with polyethylene strip, rubber or raffia.

The pots can now be plunged into peat in the grafting case at a temperature of 20°C and sprayed overhead.

Rhododendrons in Amenity Horticulture

The term 'amenity horticulture' is used in reference to local authorities, government bodies and similar establishments which are responsible for the provision and maintenance of landscaped or recreational areas.

Problems Associated with Amenity Horticulture

Apart from parks, and possibly a few other exceptions, most local authority parks departments have very little choice as far as sites are concerned. Most frequently, the areas for which they become responsible are left after the completion of housing schemes, shopping centres and roads. Often the remains of the building works are still visible, e.g. concrete, rubble, lumps of tar and mountains of sticky wet subsoil. Pollution can also be a problem in built-up and industrialised areas.

AIR POLLUTION

Luckily, with the introduction of smokeless zones, more stringent factory emission control regulations and increasingly effective monitoring devices, air pollution is on the decline.

The type of pollution is, of course, important and a slightly higher than normal percentage of sulphur in the atmosphere will do very little, if any, harm to rhododendrons. In some instances it can actually be beneficial since this element is a constituent of several of the older fungicides. It is interesting to note that, in some larger cities, cleaner air has led to a marked increase in the disease of roses known as black spot, which is due to a fungal pathogen. On the other hand, there are many strong heavy metal acids which are still being emitted, either accidentally or on purpose, and these have been known to cause brown scorch marks on many plants, including rhododendrons. Rhododendrons, however, are no more susceptible to this kind of pollution than many other plants, unless it is prolonged or severe, so it is worth attempting to grow at least some species and hybrids.

Soil pollution is a frequent cause of failure in many species. The most common pollutant is probably diesel oil. On many building sites, heavy construction equipment is fueled from barrels, with very little care being given to the amount of spillage which occurs; also generators or compressors can run for weeks with persistent leaks.

Because of the capillary action in the soil, these contaminants can move both downwards and sideways for considerable distances. Subsequently, if the architect's schedule is carried out as it should be, up to 10 cm of topsoil may be added before the horticulturists are given the ground for planting. Even assuming that the pH is satisfactory and the correct amount of peat, etc, is added, it is highly unlikely that any contamination of the subsoil will be discovered. Two things can then happen, either small plants are put directly into the topsoil or, in a site where larger specimens are being used, some of the topsoil may be excavated and replaced with good quality topsoil. In the former case, damage may take a year or two to show up; in the latter, the symptoms may appear within a few weeks as the diesel oil moves sideways from the subsoil with the natural water movement.

The symptoms are similar to attack by certain weedkillers and this can make detection of the true cause difficult, for there may have been no applications of weedkiller anywhere near the planting.

Another situation to beware of is the case where topsoil has been stored adjacent to building sites or construction yards. Very often this soil has been contaminated by spillage, but the fuel has been carried for considerable distances by seepage. The problem is that only parts of certain soil loads may be affected and therefore only the few isolated plants which are actually in contact with the material will show any symptoms. Replanting will of course have very little effect, but another death could indicate the cause of the problem. The only remedy is complete removal of all soil in the immediate vicinity.

GAS POLLUTION

Gas pollution is often encountered in town landscaping. Old or leaking gas pipes which have been disturbed by building operations can continue to discharge gas into the adjacent soil for many months after they have been disconnected. The resulting symptoms are blueing and death of the foliage. If gas is suspected, the local gas board has all the necessary equipment for detecting the leaks.

Vandalism is another problem which many local authorities have to contend with and one which tends to deter them from using the more expensive species of plants. This is perhaps one of the principal reasons why the general public do not realise that there are more hybrids than 'Pink Pearl', or more species than *R. ponticum*. To be fair, the rhododendron has neither the defensive spines of the berberis nor the rose, nor the powers of rapid regrowth found in such shrubs as the elder or broom. *R. ponticum* however, once established, will resist most damage. The top growth may have to be removed but suckering will clothe the stumps within a year or two.

I can recommend few other species for particularly vulnerable situations but there are several hybrids which are reasonably vigorous and will recover after being trodden on. Several cultivars of the smaller evergreen Azalea group have been successfully established in raised beds in the middle of a housing scheme, while *R*. 'Elizabeth', in possibly one of the largest plantings of the cultivar in the west of Scotland, is thriving, alongside *R*. 'Sappho', adjacent to a busy trunk road in an industrial town.

Parks

Usually, local authority parks have been either inherited in a more or less established condition, from local landowners, or designed purposely by one of the famous landscape gardeners, such as Joseph Paxton. Two styles of rhododendron collection have therefore emerged.

Pollok in Glasgow was an old estate inherited from Sir John Stirling Maxwell. Its rhododendron collection took a lifetime to build and contains some of the original material imported into the British Isles. Unfortunately, in this particular instance, the collection is undoubtedly declining due to the lack of specialist knowledge and enthusiasm required to maintain the specimens in a vigorous condition. There are probably many more such examples throughout the world and I feel that it should be incumbent on local authorities to follow the examples set by the various National Trusts in maintaining these collections for posterity.

In the case of mature parkland, where large plantings of old hybrids have often been allowed to deteriorate to such an extent that the root stock, invariably *R. ponticum*, has almost totally taken over, the impression is given that the Victorians must have had a somewhat limited choice of plant material. This was not the case and occasionally an example of fine old specimens in pristine condition can be found.

While appreciating that very few local authorities are well endowed financially, I feel quite strongly that proper programmes of restoration should be implemented. It is neither necessary nor particularly desirable to totally rebuild a collection in a few years but if a small sum were to be laid aside each year for plant material, a significant amount of replanting could be carried out.

Use of Rhododendrons in Civic Decorations

Virtually all local authorities have at least one nursery unit which provides plant material for civic decorations. Rhododendrons, fortunately, can make superb pot-plants, given the correct basic attention.

CHOICE OF SPECIES OR CULTIVAR

Rhododendrons are not difficult to transplant and it may come as little surprise to learn that many species and hybrids make excellent long-lived pot-plants, for use as permanent displays, in exhibitions, or as decorations.

The best types to select belong to the wide range of small (rather than dwarf, which are too easily stolen) to medium-sized early-flowering species or hybrids.

The ubiquitous and excellent hybrid *R*. 'Elizabeth' will complement *R*. 'Blue Diamond' well and both flower in late spring. *R*. x *praecox* looks particularly well against a background of yellow narcissus. There are literally hundreds from which to choose but general habit and the clarity of flower colour are the most important considerations. Avoid the tall straggly species and those with large trusses of flowers as these tend to be damaged rather easily. Remember that you may not always have complete control over the way in which they are handled.

PREPARATION FOR DISPLAY

Specimens must never be allowed to run short of water at any time, either before, during or after flowering. As the specimens selected will probably be fairly hardy, any protection given to them in the greenhouse during the early part of the year must be combined with maximum ventilation at all times, except during severe frost or high winds. (High winds will cause structural damage to the greenhouse otherwise.) Heat can be employed to advance the flowering date, but as the light levels are low during the early part of the year, the temperature should not be increased to more than 5–10°C above that outside. *R. simsii* (the so-called *Azalea indica*) is often forced commercially at considerably higher temperatures, but it invariably suffers as a result in later months.

CONTAINERS

Most of the semi-rigid plastic containers currently available are suitable. A maximum diameter of 30 cm will allow for ease of handling. Drainage holes are essential, as hoses are normally used both indoors and out during the summer and waterlogging can present quite a problem. After several years the plants will outgrow the containers and the best specimens can then be planted out in the nursery for use as stock plants.

Greenhouse Borders

Direct planting into greenhouse borders is carried out very effectively in many of the larger botanic gardens and there is no reason, other than perhaps the lack of a suitable greenhouse, that the same should not happen in a local authority display unit. This enables the more tender species to be grown.

Species of the Maddenia and Edgeworthia subsections (Maddenii and Edgworthii series) are possibly the most commonly seen in these situations.

The Malesian species, however, in particular, deserve to be grown more than they are at present and they would possibly rival even the orchid as a talking point for the thousands of visitors who regularly stroll through the larger parks. Few nurseries, however, offer these species for sale. While the Malesian species prefer warmer temperatures than the more familiar hardy types, their general culture is similar, although frequent damping down of foliage and shading from the sun are prerequisites to the healthy growth of this exceedingly unusual and sometimes most un-rhododendron-like group.

Appendix 1
Species Generally Available from the Nursery Trade

The following species are generally obtainable from the leading nurseries, although it is unlikely that any one nursery will grow all the species listed. The plants available will vary from year to year, depending on the grower's success in propagating some of the more difficult-to-root species. In general, the plants should be correctly labelled, but if you have any doubts about their authenticity it is advisable to inform the nursery immediately. The names do, however, change and many nurseries are still growing plants classified under older taxonomy. This can be checked in various publications but the latest edition of the *Rhododendron Handbook* published by the Royal Horticultural Society is a recommended authority.

The 1980 Handbook lists the major changes in taxonomy of the *Rhododendron,* which are currently being proposed by Drs Cullen and Chamberlain of the Royal Botanic Gardens, Edinburgh, and if these are fully accepted in the horticultural world, nursery catalogues may change considerably over the next few years.

The following lists do not represent a complete catalogue of all species either available or offered for sale.

Key to symbols:

* proposed name changes
l species which will grow fairly large but nevertheless are worth growing in the smaller garden due to the value of their flowers or foliage.

HARDINESS (R.H.S. CLASSIFICATION)

H1 normally requiring greenhouse protection
H2 requiring protection even in the most sheltered gardens

H3 hardy in the west and in favoured areas in the south and east of the
        British Isles
H4 hardy throughout the British Isles

HARDINESS (AMERICAN RATING)

H–1 hardy to − 31.6°C
H–2 hardy to − 26°C
H–3 hardy to − 20.5°C
H–4 hardy to − 15°C
H–5 hardy to − 9.5°C
In practice, the rating refers to the ability of the plant to withstand cold
rather than heat. The American rating, like the British system, should be
regarded as a guide rather than the rule. The two systems should on no
account be confused as they are virtually opposite in meaning.

FLOWERS

F1–4 in ascending order of their value and beauty. This form of
classification has been discarded in the latest edition of the *Rhododendron
Handbook*.

LEAVES

L1–4 in ascending order of their value and beauty. The latest edition of
the *Rhodendron Handbook* has discarded this form of classification as well.

HABIT

  c = compact
  d = dwarf
  m = medium
  p = prostrate
 .s = straggling
  t = tall
Although, once again, the Royal Horticultural Society has decided to
omit this classification, I feel it gives the enthusiast an idea of the habit
which the plant will eventually adopt, and therefore helps in the planning
of its final position in the garden.

FLOWER COLOUR

Flower colour will almost certainly vary from form to form, and it is therefore essential to purchase or propagate only that clone which you have seen in flower.

FLOWERING TIME

This will depend primarily on the season, but clonal variations and locality will also play an important part in the flowering period. There will be six months difference between the flowering periods in the northern and southern hemispheres.

Species Suitable for the Rock Garden, Small Garden or Peat Walls

Species	Hardiness American (R.H.S.)	Flower colour/merit	Date of Flowering	Leaf/ merit	Habit
alabamense	H–3–4	white F1–2	April-May	L1–2	d-m
anthopogon	H–4	cream-pink F2–3	April	L1	d
aperantum	H–4(H3)	white-red	April-May	L1	d
atlanticum	H–4	white-pink	May	L1–2	d-m
auritum	H–2–3(H5)	yellow F2–3	April	L1–2	d
bakeri	H–3–4	orange, red, yellow F2–3	June	L1–2	d-m
brachyanthum	H–4	pale yellow F1–3	June-July	L1–2	d
caesium	H–4	green, yellow F1–2	May-June	L1–2	d
calostrotum	H–4(H3)	pink, purple, red F2–4	April-June	L1–2	d
campylogynum	H3–4(H2)	pale pink-dark purple F2–3	May-June	L2–3	d
campylogynum var. myrtilloides	H–3–4(H2)	plum, pink, white F3	May-June	L2–3	d
camtschaticum	H–4(H2)	reddish purple F2–3	May-June	L1–2	d
canadense	H–4	rose-purple, white F2–3	April	L1	d
capitatum	H–4	white-pink F1–2	March-May	L1	d
cephalanthum	H–4	white F2–3	April-May	L1–2	d
chamaethomsonii	H–4	red, pink, white F2–3	March-April	L1–2	d
*chrysanthum	H–4(H3)	yellow F1–2	May-June	L1–2	d
ciliatum	H–3–4	pink, white F2–3	March-May	L1–2	d-m
complexum	H–4	rosy-purple	April-May	L1–2	d
*degronianum	H–4(H3)	pink F1–2	May	L2–3	m,c
*drumonium	H–4(H3)	purple	April-May	L2–3	d,c
fastigiatum	H–4(H2)	purple, blue F2–3	April-May	L1–2	d,c

Species	Hardiness R.H.S. (American)	Flower colour/merit	Date of flowering	Leaf/ merit	Habit
ferrugineum	H–4(H2)	rosy-crimson F1–2	June–July	L1–2	d-m,s
flavidum	H–4(H2)	pale yellow F2–3	March–May	L1–2	d
fletcheranum	H–4	white, rose F2–3	March–May	L1–2	
forrestii	H–4(H3)	scarlet F1–4	April–May	L1–2	d,p
forrestii repens	H–4(H3)	scarlet F1–4	April–May	L1–2	d,p
glaucophyllum	H–3–4(H3)	pink, pinkish, purple F2–3	April–May	L1–2	d-m
*glomerulatum	H–4(H3)	purple-mauve F1–2	April–May	L1–2	d
hanceanum	H–4	white-yellow F2–3	April	L1–2	d-m
hippophaeoides	H–4(H3)	blue-pink F2–3	March–May	L2–3	d-m
hirsutum	H–4(H2)	pink-red F1–2	June–July	L1–2	d-m
impeditum	H–4(H2)	mauve-purplish blue F3–4	April–May	L1–2	d
*imperator	H–3–4(H3)	pink, pinkish-purple	April–May	L1–2	d,p
intricatum	H–4(H2)	lilac-mauve F2–3	March–May	L1–2	d
keiskei	H–3–4(H2)	lemon-yellow F2–3	April–May	L1–2	d-m,c
*keleticum	H–4(H2)	purplish-crimson F1–3	May–June	L1–2	d,p
kongboense	H–4	bright rose F1–2	March–May	L1–2	d
lepidostylum	H–4	pale yellow F1	May–June	L3–4	d
lepidotum	H–3–4(H3)	pink, purple, crimson, yellow, white	May–June	L1–2	d-m
leucaspis	H–3–4(H4)	white F3–4	Feb.–April	L2–3	d
linearifolium	H–3–4	pink F1	April–May	L1–2	d-m
linearifolium macrosepalum	H–3	lilac-pink, rose-purple F1–2	April–May	L1–2	d-m
lowndesii	H–3–4	pale yellow, spotted carmine F1–2	May–July	L1	d
ludlowii	H–4	yellow, spotted red, brown F2–3	April–May	L1	d
megeratum	H–3–4(H4)	yellow F2–3	March–April	L1–2	d
mekongense	H–4	pale yellow F1–2	May	L1–2	d-m
microleucum	H–4(H2)	white F3	April–May	L2	d
moupinense	H–3–4(H4)	white, pink, rose F3–4	Feb.–March	L1–2	d-m
nivale	H–4	purple, mauve, violet F1	April–May	L1	d
obtusum	H–3–4	red F2–3	May	L1–2	d-m
orthocladum	H–4	pale mauve F1–2	April–May	L1–2	d-m
*patulum	H–4	crimson-purple F2–3	April–May	L1–2	d,p
pemakoense	H–3–4(H3)	purple, pink F2–3	March–April	L1–2	d
primuliflorum	H–4	yellow, white, rose F2–3	April–May	L1–2	d-m
pumilum	H–3–4	pink-rose F1–3	May–June	L1–2	d
racemosum	H–4(H2)	pink-deep rose F1–3	March–May	L1–2	d-m
*radicans	H–4(H3)	purple F2–3	May–June	L2–3	d,p

Species	Hardiness R.H.S. (American)	Flower colour/merit	Date of flowering	Leaf/ merit	Habit
ramosissimum	H–4	purplish red-blue F1–2	April-May	L1–2	d
roxieanum	H–4	white F2–3	April-May	L2–3	d-m
rupicola	H–4	deep blue-purple F3–4	April-May	L1–2	d
russatum	H–4	blue-purple F3–4	April-May	L1–2	d
sanguineum	H–4(H3)	bright crimson F1–3	March-May	L1–2	d
sargentianum	H–4(H3)	lemon-yellow, white F2–3	April-June	L1–2	d
scintillans	H–4(H3)	purple-blue F2–4	April-May	L1–2	d
serpyllifolium	H–3–4	rosy-pink F1	April-May	L1–2	d
shweliense	H–4(H3)	pink tinged yellow F1–2	April-June	L1–2	d
tapetiforme	H–4	rose-purple, blue-purple, pink F1–2	April	L1–2	d
trichostomum	H–3–4(H4)	rose-white F2–3	May-June	L1–2	d
*tsangpoense	H–4	pink, purple, crimson, violet F2–3	April-June	L1–2	d
tsariense	H–4	pink, cream, white F1–2	March-May	L2–3	d-m
uniflorum	H–4	pink-purple F2–3	April-May	L1	d
valentinianum	H–3(H5)	yellow F2–3	March-April	L1–2	d
viridescens	H–4	yellowish-green F1–2	May-June	L1–2	
williamsianum	H–3–4(H3)	shell pink F2–3	April	L2–3	d-m
yakushimanum	H–4(H3)	pink-white F3–4	May	L2–3	d-m

Species Suitable for the Medium-Sized Garden

Species	Hardiness American (R.H.S.)	Flower colour/merit	Date of flowering	Leaf/ merit	Habit
aberconwayi	H4	white F2–4	April-May	L1–2	m
adenogynum	H4(H–2)	magenta-red, purple F2	April-May	L2	m
*adenophorum	H4	rose F1–2	April-May	L2–3	m
l albrechtii	H4	deep rose F3–4	April-May	L1–2	m,c
l amagianum	H4	orange-red F3	June-July	L2–3	m-t
annae	H3–4	white, flushed rose F1–2	May-June	L1–2	m
*astrocalyx augustinii	H3–4(H–3)	very variable pink-blue F2–4	April-May	L1–2	m-t
baileyi	H3–4(H–4)	purple F2–3	April-May	L1	d-m
beanianum	H3–4(H–4)	crimson F1–3	March-May	L2–3	m,s
*bodinieri	H3–4	rose, purple spots F2–3	March-April	L1–2	m
brachycarpum	H4(H–2)	white-yellow F2–3	June-July	L1–2	m
brevistylum	H4(H–4)	rose, crimson marks F2–3	late June-July	L1–2	m
bureavii	H4(H–2)	white, rose, crimson markings F2–3	April-May	L3–4	m

Species	Hardiness R.H.S. (American)	Flower colour/merit	Date of flowering	Leaf/ merit	Habit
calendulaceum	H4	yellow, orange, scarlet F2–4	May-June	L1–2	m
callimorphum	H3–4(H–4)	rose F3–4	April-May	L2–3	m
campylocarpum	H3–4(H–3)	yellow, white F3–4	April-May	L1–2	m
*carolinianum	H4(H–2)	purple, pink F2–3	May-June	L2	m
caucasicum	H4(H–3)	yellow, white F1–2	April-May	L1–2	m
cerasinum	H4	red, white F1–3	May-June	L1–2	m
*chaetomallum	H4(H–4)	crimson, rose F2–3	March-May	L2–3	m
*chapmanii	H4(H–3)	rose F2–3	April-May	L1–2	m
chlorops	H4	cream, pale yellow F2–3	May	L1–2	m
cinnabarinum	H4(H–3)	cinnabar-red F3–4	April-July	L2–3	m-t
cinnabarinum roylei	H4	plum-crimson F3–4	April-July	L2–3	m-t
collettianum	H3	white, tinged rose F1–2	May	L1–2	m
*concatenans	H4	apricot F2–3	April-May	L2–3	m
concinnum coxianum	H4(H–3)	purple, white F1–2	April-May	L1–2	m
*crassum	H2–4(H–5)	white-pink F2–3	June-July	L2–3	m
crinigerum	H4(H–2)	white, crimson blotch F2–3	April-May	L2–3	m
l dauricum	H4(H–2)	rose-purple F2–3	Jan.-March	L1–2	m,c
davidsonianum	H3–4(H–4)	rose-purple, white F2–4	April-May	L1–2	m
detonsum	H4	rose-pink F1–3	May	L1–3	m
dichroanthum	H4(H–4)	orange-pink F1–3	May-June	L1–2	m
eclecteum	H4(H–3)	white, yellow, pink F1–3	Jan.-April	L2–3	m
*eriogynum	H2–3(H–4)	red F3–4	June	L2–3	m-t
erythrocalyx	H4	white, pink F1–2	April-May	L2–3	m
floccigerum	H4(H–3)	crimson, yellow, rose F1–3	March-April	L1–2	m
formosanum	H4	white-pink	March-April		
formosum	H2	white/yellow and rose F3–4	May-June	L1–2	m,s
fulgens	H4(H–3)	scarlet F1–3	Feb.-April	L1–2	m
genesterianum	H2–3	purple F1–2	April	L2–3	m
griersonianum	H3–4(H–5)	scarlet F3–4	June	L2–3	m,s
habrotrichum	H4(H–4)	white, pale rose	April	L2–3	m
haematodes	H4(H–4)	scarlet	May-June	L3–4	m
*hardingii	H2–3	white flushed pink F1–2	April-May	F1–2	m,s
heliolepis	H4(H–3)	purple, pink, white F1–3	June-July	L1–2	m-t
hookeri	H3–4	red, pink F2–4	March-April	L2–3	m-t
horlickianum	H1	white	April		
hunnewellianum	H3–4	white, pink	March-April		
hyperythrum	H3–4	white-pink F2–3	April-May	L2–3	m-t
indicum	H2–3	red F2–3	June-July	L1–2	d-m,p
insigne	H4(H–4)	pink-white F3–4	May-June	L3–4	m
japonicum	H4	orange-red F3–4	May	L1–2	d-m
johnstoneanum	H2–3(H–4)	yellow-white F3–4	April-May	L1–2	m-t
keysii	H3–4(H–4)	red, orange F2–3	June-July	L1–2	m,s
lanatum	H4	yellow F2–3	April-May	L2–3	m

115

Species	Hardiness R.H.S. (American)	Flower colour/merit	Date of flowering	Leaf/ merit	Habit
lindleyi	H1–3(H–6)	cream with yellow or orange blotch F4	May-June	L2–3	m,s
*litiense	H4(H–4)	yellow F2–3	May-June	L2–3	m
lopsanguineum	H3–4	crimson F1–3	April	L2–3	m
lutescens	H3–4(H–4)	yellow F1–2	March-April	L1–2	m
luteum	H4	yellow F3–4	May-June	L2–3	m
lyi	H2–3	white, yellow blotch F2–3	April-June	L2–3	m
*makinoi	H3–4(H–3)	pink F2–3	May-June	L2–3	m
martinianum	H4	rose, white F2–3	April-May	L1–2	m
meddianum	H3–4	scarlet F2–4	April	L2–3	m
megacalyx	H2–3(H–6)	white F3–4	April-June	L1–2	m,s-t
*metternichii	H4	rose F2–3	April-May	L2–3	m
minus	H4(H–2)	pink, white F1–2	May-June	L1–2	m
mucronulatum	H4(H–2)	rosy-purple F2–3	Jan.-March	L1–2	m
neriiflorum	H3–4(H–4)	crimson F3–4	April-May	L1–2	m,s
nudiflorum	H4	white, pink, red F1–2	May	L1–2	m
oblongifolium	H3	white, pink F1–2	June-July	L1–2	m
occidentale	H4	white, pink, yellow blotch F2–3	June	L1–2	m
oldhamii	H2–3	red F2–3	May	L1–2	m
orbiculare	H4(H–3)	pink F2–3	March-April	L2–3	m
pentaphyllum	H4	rose-pink F3	March-April	L2–3	m
polyandrum	H2–3(H–6)	white-yellow F2–4	May-June	L2–3	m,s
polylepis	H4(H–3)	purple F1–2	April	L1–2	m
pseudochrysanthum	H4	pink, white F3–4	April	L2–3	m
pseudoyanthinum see concinnum					
pubescens	H4(H–3)	rose, pinkish-white F2–3	April-May	L1–2	m
pulchrum	H3	rose-purple F2–3	May	L1–2	m
reticulatum	H4	rose-purple F2–3	April-May	L1–2	m-t
rigidum	H4	rose-lavender, white F1–3	March-May	L1–2	m
roseum	H4	pink-red F2–3	May	L1–2	m
scabrum	H2	rose-red, scarlet F2–3	April-May	L1–2	m
l schippenbachii	H4	pink F3–4	April-May	L2–3	m
searsiae	H4(H–3)	white, rose, mauve F1–2	April-May	L1–2	m
semibarbatum	H4	white F1	June	L1–2	m
sherriffii	H4	carmine F1–3	April	L1–2	m
smirnowii	H4(H–2)	rose-purple F2–3	May-June	L2–3	m
souliei	H4(H–3)	white, rose F2–4	May	L2–3	m
taggianum	H1–2(H–6)	white, pale yellow blotch F4	April-May	L1–2	m,s
taliense	H4	yellow, cream F1–2	April-May	L1–2	m
triflorum	H4(H–3)	lemon-yellow, pink F1–2	May-June	L1–2	m
vaseyi	H4	pink, white, with red spots	April-May	L1–2	m
venator	H3–4(H–4)	scarlet, reddish orange F2–3	May-June	L1–2	m

Species	Hardiness American (R.H.S.)	Flower colour/merit	Date of flowering	Leaf/merit	Habit
viscosum	H4	white, F2–3	June-July	L1–2	m
*viscidifolium	H3–4	red	April-May		m
wallichii	H4	lilac spotted rose F1–3	April	L1–2	m
wardii	H4(H–4)	yellow F2–4	May	L2–3	m-t
wasonii	H4	white, pink, yellow F1–3	May	L2–3	m
weyrichii	H4	red F2–3	April-May	L1–2	m
wightii	H3–4	yellow F2–3	April-May	L2–3	m-t,s
wilsonae	H1–2(H–3)	pink F1–2	April	L1–2	m
wiltonii	H4	white, pink F2–3	April-May	L2–3	m
*xanthocodon	H4(H–3)	cream-yellow F2–3	May	L2–3	m
yunnanense	H4(H–3)	pink, white, lavender F2–4	May	L1–2	m
zaleucum	H3–4	white, pink, purple, yellow F2–3	April	L1–2	m-t

Species Suitable for a Large Garden

Species	Hardiness R.H.S. (American)	Flower colour/merit	Date of flowering	Leaf/merit	Habit
ambiguum	H4(H–4)	yellow F2–3	April-May	L1	m-t
*anwheiense	H4	white, red spots F1–2	April-May	L1–2	m
argyrophyllum	H4(H–3)	white, pink F3–4	May	L2–3	m-t
*arizelum	H3–4(H–4)	yellow, pink F2–3	April-May	L3–4	m-t
auriculatum	H4(H–3)	white, pink F2–3	July-Sept.	L2–4	m-t
barbatum	H3–4(H–4)	scarlet F3–4	March-April	L2–3	t
basilicum	H3–4(H–3)	yellow, cream F2–3	April-May	L2–3	t
beesianum	H3–4(H–2)	pink, white F1–3	April-May	L2–3	t
calophytum	H4(H–3)	white F2–3	March-April	L2–4	t
campanulatum	H3–4(H–2)	blue, purple, plum, white F1–4	April-May	L2–4	m-t
catawbiense	H4(H–1)	purple, pink, white F1–2	May-June	L1–2	m-t
coriaceum	H3–4(H–4)	white, rose, spotted F2–3	April	L2–3	t
cyanocarpum	H4(H–4)	pink, white F2–3	March-April	L2–3	m-t
decorum	H3–4(H–4)	white, tinged pink or green F2–3	May-June	L2–3	m-t
*delavayi	H2–3(H–5)	red F2–4	March-May	L2–3	m-t
*desquamatum	H3–4(H–3)	pink, purple F2–3	April-May	L1–2	m-t
diaprepes	H3(H–4)	white, rose F2–3	June-July	L2–3	m-t
*discolor	H3–4(H–3)	white, pink F2–4	June-July	L2–3	m-t
ellipticum	H2–3	rose	March-May		
*eximium	H3–4(H–4)	rose	April-May	L3–4	m-t
falconeri	H3–4(H–4)	yellow, white, pink F3–4	April-May	L3–4	m-t

Species	Hardiness American (R.H.S.)	Flower colour/merit	Date of flowering	Leaf/merit	Habit
*fictolacteum	H4(H–3)	white F2–4	April-May	L2–3	m-t
floribundum	H4	lavender F1–3	April	L2–3	m-t
fortunei	H4(H–2)	pink F3–4	May	L1–3	m-t
fulvum	H4(H–4)	white-pink F2–4	March-May	L2–4	m-t
hemsleyanum	H3–4	white F2–3	May-June	L2–3	m-t
hirtipes	H3–4	pink, white F1–3	April	L1–3	m-t
hodgsonii	H4(H–4)	crimson, pink, purple F2–3	April-May	L2–3	m-t
*hypoglaucum	H4	white F1–3	May-June	L1–2	m-t
irroratum	H3–4(H–4)	white, pink F2–4	March-May	L2–3	m-t
lanigerum	H4	purple-magenta F3–4	March-April	L2–3	m-t
macabeanum	H3–4(H–4)	yellow F3–4	March-May	L3–4	m-t
maculiferum	H4	white, rose F2–3	April	L1–2	m-t
magnificum	H2–3	rosy-purple F2–4	Feb.-April	L3–4	m-t
mallotum	H3–4(H–4)	crimson F2–4	March-April	L3–4	m-t
mollyanum (now montroseanum)	H2–3	deep pink F2–4	March-May	L3–4	m-t
morii	H3–4	white, rose F2–3	April-May	L1–2	m-t
niveum	H3–4	blue-lilac F2–4	April-May	L2–3	m-t
oreodoxa	H4(H–3)	pink F1–3	March-April	L2–3	m-t
oreotrephes	H4(H–3)	pink-purple F1–3	April-May	L1–2	m-t
pachysanthum	H4	white	April		
ponticum	H4(H–3)	purple F1–3	June-July	L1–3	m-t
preptum	H3–4	white F2–3	April-May	L2–3	m
*puralbum	H4	white F2–3	May	L2–3	m
rex	H4	pink, white F3–4	April-May	L3–4	m-t
rubiginosum	H4(H–2)	lilac, pink F2–3	April-May	L1–2	m-t
rufum	H4	white, purple F1–2	April	L1–3	m
sinogrande	H3–4(H–4)	pale yellow, white F3–4	April-May	L4	m-t
sutchuenense	H4(H–3)	pink, lilac F2–4	Feb.-April	L2–3	m-t
thayerianum	H4	pink, white F2–3	June-July	L2–3	m-t
thomsonii	H3–4(H–3)	red F3–4	April-May	L2–3	m-t
traillianum	H4	white, rose F1–3	April-May	L2–3	m-t
trichanthum	H4	purple F1–2	May-June	L1–2	m-t
vellereum	H4	white, rose F2–3	April	L1–2	m
vernicosum	H3–4(H–3)	white, rose F1–3	May	L2–3	m-t

Hybrids for the Rock Garden, Small Garden and Peat Walls

Name	Parents	Hardiness R.H.S.	Flower colour/merit	Date of flowerin
Augfast	augustinii x fastigiatum	H4	deep blue F4	May
'Blue Diamond'	augustinii x 'Intrifast'	H4	mauve blue F4	April
'Bow-Bells'	'Corona' x williamsianum	H4	pink F4	April

Name	Parents	Hardiness R.H.S.	Flower colour/merit	Date of flowering
'Carmen'	*forrestii repens* x			
	sanguineum didymum	H4	scarlet F4	May
Cilpinense	*ciliatum* x *moupinense*	H4	pink-white F4	March
'Doncaster'	*arboreum* x	H4	red F4	May
'Elisabeth Hobbie'	'Essex Scarlet' x *forrestii repens*	H4	scarlet F4	May
'Elizabeth'	*forrestii repens* x *griersonianum*	H4	scarlet F4	April
Fabia	*dichroanthum* x *griersonianum*	H4	orange, pink F2	May
'Humming Bird'	*haematodes* x *williamsianum*	H3	pink, crimson F2	May
'Pink Drift'	*calostrotum* x *scintillans*	H4	pink F4	May
x *praecox*	*ciliatum* x *dauricum*	H4	purple, pink F4	Feb.-March
Princess Anne	*hanceanum* x *keiskei*	H4	yellow F4	May
Ptarmigan .	*leucaspis* x *microleucum*	H4	white F4	May
Racil	*ciliatum* x *racemosum*	H4	pink F4	May
Sarled	*sargentianum* x			
	trichostomum ledoides	H4	white F3	May
'Scarlet Wonder'	*forrestii repens* x *williamsianum*	H4	scarlet F3	May
'Seta'	*moupinense* x *spinuliferum*	H4	pink and white F4	Jan.-March
'Yellowhammer'	*flavidum* x *sulphureum*	H4	yellow F4	April

In addition most of the evergreen 'azalea' types such as 'Malvaticum', 'Kaempferi' and Vuyk hybrids would be excellent.

The above list represents only a small fraction of those available commercially and is only a personal choice.

Hybrids for the Medium-Sized Garden

Name	Parents	Hardiness R.H.S.	Flower colour/merit	Date of flowering
'Adriaan Koster'	*campylocarpum* hybrid x			
	'Mrs Lindsay Smith'	H4	cream, yellow F4	May
'Bagshot Ruby'	*thomsonii* x	H4	crimson F3	May
'Britannia'	'Queen Wilhelmina' x			
	'Stanley Davies'	H4	cerise-scarlet F4	May
Chev.F.de Sauvage		H4	red F2	April-May
'Christmas Cheer'	*caucasicum* hybrid	H4	pink F4	Jan.-March
Conroy	*cinnabarinum roylei* x			
	concatenans	H3	orange F3	May
'Corona'		H4	coral-pink F4	May
'Countess of Haddington'	*ciliatum* x *dalhousiae*	H2	pink, scented, yellow F4	May
Damaris 'Logan'	*camplyocarpum* x 'Dr Stocker'	H3	yellow F4	May
'Dive'	*griersonianum* x 'Ladybird'	H4	scarlet F3	June
'Harvest Moon'	*campylocarpum* hybrid x			
	'Mrs Lindsay Smith'	H4	cream, crimson blotch F3	May

Name	Parents	Hardiness R.H.S.	Flower colour/merit	Date of flowering
Lady Bessborough	*campylocarpum elatum* x *discolor*	H4	yellow F4	May
'Mount Everest'	*campanulatum* x *griffithianum*	H4	white F4	May

Hybrids for the Large Garden

Name	Parents	Hardiness R.H.S.	Flower colour/merit	Date of flowering
'Angelo'	*discolor* x *griffithianum*	H3	white, scented F4	July
'Beauty of Littleworth'	*griffithianum* hybrid	H4	white, red spots F4	April
'Cinnkeys'	*cinnabarinum* x *keysii*	H4	red-tipped orange F3	May
'Cornish Cross'	*griffithianum* x *thomsonii*	H3	scarlet-pink F4	May
'Crest'	Lady Bessborough x *wardii*	H3	yellow F3–4	May
'Cynthia'	*catawbiense* x *griffithianum*	H4	rose-crimson F4	May
'Earl of Donoughmore'	*griersonianum* x	H4	light red F4	June
'Fastuosum Flore Pleno'	*catawbiense* x *ponticum*	H4	lilac, semi-double F4	June
'Fusilier'	*elliottii* x *griersonianum*	H3	scarlet F4	July
'Goldfort'	*fortunei* x 'Goldsworth yellow'	H4	creamy yellow F4	May
'Goldsworth Crimson'	'Doncaster' x *griffithianum*	H4	crimson F4	April
Lady Roseberry	*cinnabarinum* x 'Royal Flush' (pink form)	H3	pink F4	May
Loderi	*fortunei* x *griffithianum*	H3	pink-white, many clones F4	May
Naomi	'Aurora' x *fortunei*	H4	lilac-pink F4	May
Nobleanum	*arboreum* x *caucasicum*	H4	pink F4	May
Olive	*dauricum* x *moupinense*	H4	lilac-rose F3	Jan.-March
'Penjerrick'	*campylocarpum elatum* x *griffithianum*	H3	pink F4	April
'Pink Pearl'	'Broughtonii' x 'George Hardy'	H4	pink F4	May
'Polar Bear'	*auriculatum* x *diaprepes*	H3	white, scented F4	July-Aug.
'Sappho'		H4	white, maroon blotch F3	May
'Susan'	*campanulatum* x *fortunei*	H4	lavender F4	April
'Tally Ho'	*eriogynum* x *griersonianum*	H3	scarlet F4	July

Appendix 2
Plants for a Purpose

Rhododendrons for Hedges

A hedge is a line of closely planted trees or shrubs generally forming a barrier around a field or garden. In ornamental horticulture, hedges are often used to channel interest or to provide decoration.

With perhaps one notable exception, the rhododendron is not often deliberately used as a hedge, as it is generally planted for the beauty of its flowers, foliage or autumn colour. Invariably, however, on an old estate, there will be a mass planting of hybrid rhododendrons which have been allowed to intermingle with one another completely. After years of neglect, the rootstock, *R. ponticum,* has taken over and the growth has become even more rampant. When these bushes are eventually cut back, in order to clear an overgrown path or otherwise gain access, a hedge will be formed incidentally. Such hedges do not generally flower. In rhododendrons, the flower buds for the following year are produced on the current year's growth and pruning during the winter months removes the potential blossom. Another factor contributing to their non-flowering condition is that, very often, these hedges are overshadowed by massive, dense forest tree species, which totally obscure the sunlight necessary for hastening the production and ripening of the flower buds.

R. ponticum is probably the only species commonly used as a hedge as, due to its rapid growth, it is resilient to pruning. With careful, selective, summer-pruning, this species can be encouraged to flower, although perhaps not profusely. This pruning operation involves the removal of about one-third of the young shoots every year until flower buds appear. In successive years, these shoots can be cut hard back once the flowering period is over. Interestingly enough, there is a magnificent hedge of *R.* x *praecox* adorning the Royal Botanic Gardens, Edinburgh. As can be seen (Plate 51), this species flowers profusely; *R. vaseyi* planted at Crarae produces a similar effect. It is possible that many more species and smaller hybrids could be treated in a similar manner.

Fragrance

Fragrance or scent is a somewhat intangible subject for, like colour, individual interpretations vary. However, in the case of colours, fairly standardised and progressive measurements exist, such as the Royal Horticultural Society Colour Chart, which at least enables colours to be compared with a series of references.

Sensitivity to smell can vary not only from person to person but also in one person at different times throughout the day. Some people can detect a certain fragrance in much lower concentrations than others and, from my own and several other people's experiences, those horticulturalists who suffer from hay fever seem at times to have an exceptionally acute sense of smell.

Fragrance in both lepidote and elepidote rhododendrons is derived from the flowers but in the lepidote group, the foliage also produces an aroma.

FRAGRANT FLOWERS

The Maddenia subsection (Maddenii series) contains probably the largest number of species known for their fragrance, the most common of these being *RR. dalhousiae, lindleyi* and *megacalyx.*

In the Edgeworthia subsection (Edgeworthii series), the type species *edgeworthii* and the hybrid *R. x fragrantissimum (edgeworthii x formosum)* are quite highly scented. In small amounts, fragrance can be, and is, regarded as desirable. Unfortunately, if large numbers of strongly scented plants are grown too close to a dwelling house, the results can be overpowering. References are often made to the similarities between the genus *Lilium* and the flowers of such species as *RR. lindleyi* and *megacalyx.* This coincidence holds true for both shape and scent.

Among the larger-growing species, natural selection has produced the subsection Fortunea with its fragrant specimens such as *RR. decorum, diaprepes, fortunei* and *griffithianum.*

For the enthusiast able to grow the Malesian group, there will be no shortage of scent in the greenhouse, as species such as *RR. superbum, konori* and *herzogii* can testify.

AROMATIC FOLIAGE

The dissemination of aroma from the foliage of the scented-leaved species can take place entirely without any physical contact. Under certain weather conditions, especially on still damp days, the air can become laden with the various scents of the many aromatic species such as *RR. campylogynum, glaucophyllum* and *cinnabarinum*. Propagation, however, will provide the greatest insight into those species and cultivars which exude pleasant (or otherwise) scents, for handling the plants will release aromas even from those which are normally a little shy to do so.

Bark Effect

While many trees and shrubs have long been renowned for the beauty of their bark, the rhododendron has, for some reason, received little attention in this respect. Since the majority of trees and shrubs with a fine bark are deciduous, the glossy reds, yellows, greens and whites of the bark are much more apparent than in rhododendrons, which tend to be evergreen. Fine foliage and flowers have detracted attention from a bark which in many instances is both interesting and attractive. *R. arboreum* subsp. *zeylanicum (R. zeylanicum)* has a fascinating gnarled bark once it has reached about 20 to 30 years old and this is, in fact, a good means of identification. No one particular subsection or series has any monopoly on types with good bark, for there is considerable variation, even within a single species.

    R. barbatum has a fine reddish to silver bark, smooth and peeling (Plate 66). Others, such as *RR. thomsonii, hodgsonii,* and *arboreum,* and certain members of the Triflora subsection, are all worth growing for this characteristic, although the plants may not develop to their full potential for several years.

Foliage Effect

As shrubs, rhododendrons would be worth growing, even if they were never to flower, for the magnificence of many species lies in the beauty of the foliage. This foliage effect can be attributed, amongst other factors, to the sheer size of the leaves, the colour of the young growth and the indumentum, and the autumnal tints. In leaf size alone, the genus varies from the minute 12 mm of *R. serpyllifolium* to the 1 m of *R. sinogrande*. It is *R. sinogrande* (Plate 68) which undoubtedly attracts the most attention since, in many west coast gardens, where the rainfall is normally more than adequate and shelter from the strong winds is provided, it is by no means uncommon to find *R. sinogrande* and other large-leaved species reaching their true dimensions.

Many experienced growers are now realising that, to produce the best foliage and avoid the tall thin specimens, which have been so often seen in the past, these plants require a more open situation than was originally thought. It should, however, not be forgotten that, while light is essential to produce good foliage and flower, shelter from the wind must be provided if damage to the leaves is to be avoided.

Young Growth

It is perhaps unfortunate that we tend to take for granted the different facets of the seasons, especially the unfurling of the young growth in spring and early autumn. The bracts of such species as *R. giganteum* (now *R. protistum* var. *giganteum*) are bright red in colour, and held vertically until the foliage elongates sufficiently to cause the sheath to burst and the bracts to reflex downwards and eventually fall.

The young growths are often referred to as 'candles' for this is just what they look like from a distance, especially when the scarlet pigmentation is at its peak. The true leaves of many species are in themselves exceedingly attractive, varying through shades of fawn, pink, gold and silver, as they slowly unfurl.

Colour

COLOUR IN THE ADULT LEAF

Many species and varieties retain the brilliance of the young leaves throughout the whole year. Two very good examples of this are *R. xanthocodon* form *concatenans* (now *R. cinnabarinum* subsp. *xanthocodon*) and *R. aeruginosum* (now *R. campanulatum* subsp. *aeruginosum*), both of which are outstanding shades of glaucous green. Not only is the upper surface of the foliage interesting, but so is the lower side especially in species such as *RR. zaleucum* and *niveum* when the wind catches the leaves and exposes their silvery colour.

INDUMENTUM

Indumentum is a woolly or hairy covering found on the foliage of many shrubs and very noticeable on some rhododendron species. The colours range through silver, yellow, orange, cinnamon brown to almost red. Propagation from different clones results in variations in the quality of the indumentum and of other characteristics from plant to plant even with the same species. This is one of the problems of being unable to view a plant prior to purchase. It is, therefore, always advisable to buy clonal forms which have First Class Certificates or Awards of Merit.

In certain species, indumentum may be present only on the young foliage and will fall as the leaf matures; in others it may persist throughout the entire life of the leaf. It is quite common to find indumentum on the underside of the leaf only, such as the yellow-cinnamon colour of *R. sperabile*, although in other species, such as the beautiful *R. bureavii*, it occurs on both the foliage and young branches. The action of the wind plays a useful part in displaying these assets, particularly those of the somewhat variable *R. fulvum*.

AUTUMNAL COLOUR

Rhododendrons fall fairly neatly into two distinct groups, the evergreen and the deciduous, and, not unexpectedly, a few of the deciduous species provide a measure of autumn colour. Strangely, the glory of the autumn tints tends to vary according to the weather conditions prevailing during any particular year. Why the weather plays such an important part in the production of colour is uncertain but it appears to be linked to temperature, rainfall and, especially, to a touch of frost at the time when the chemical composition of the leaves is correctly balanced.

In the British Isles a really good season for autumn colour occurs about once every 3 or 4 years, although the intermediate years can be, and usually are, quite acceptable. In the United States of America and Canada, good colouring is a somewhat more predictable phenomenon.

Using the older classification, the deciduous species come within the heading of the 'Azalea series' with *R. luteum* probably being the chief contender for the title of best autumn colour (Plate 23). Not every plant in any one large garden will respond in exactly the same manner or to the same extent as its close neighbour. This will be due probably to a fractional difference in the micro-climate. The foliage usually changes from green through yellow to bronze, red or scarlet, and is displayed to its best when shafts of sunlight shining through the trees highlight the individual plants.

The Unopened Bud

There are two fairly distinct types of bud in rhododendrons and there should be little difficulty in telling them apart. The flower buds are generally globe-shaped whereas the growth buds are pointed. Normally, the flower buds also exhibit several interesting characteristics, which may help in the identification of the species. These buds are often covered either in woolly indumentum or in a white or silvery meal, as in *R. niveum,* which is particularly handsome, with its orange yellow colouration shining through the white mealy down of the bud. Several other species, especially the large-leaved types have flower and growth buds of particular beauty.

Leaf Scales

The lepidote section of the genus has many species which are particularly well-endowed with orange or brown scales, present not only on the foliage but also commonly on the stems, young buds and flowers. Unlike some of the other characteristics, this feature is perhaps less obvious since the individual scales are so small. However, the contrast of brown scales on a silver background can nevertheless be quite attractive, e.g. several species of the Triflora subsection.

Hairs and Bristles

The presence of hairs and bristles on both the foliage and stems of many species is another feature of interest which ought not to be overlooked. *R. ciliatum,* as its name implies, is a prime example of a rather hirsute specimen. This species and a few close relatives are fairly easily identifiable. The new subsection known as Barbata contains many species with rather beautiful long bristles, indeed the English translation of the Latin name means 'bearded'. When covered in droplets of rain or dew, these hairs glisten most attractively.

Rhododendrons for the Rock Garden

The use of rhododendrons in the rock garden is certainly to be recommended, although it is important that the pH level of the soil is checked prior to planting. Where an old rock garden is being renovated, there may well be pockets of high pH soil, especially where plants such as *Dianthus* have been growing, for various forms of limestone might have been added to reduce the acidity of the soil and make it more suitable for this type of plant. Although a rock garden may be constructed from limestone, as long as the limestone is not readily broken down by the action of water and wind, it should be suitable for rhododendrons. If there is any doubt, consult a local horticultural adviser or agricultural college. Good drainage and an adequate supply of moisture are essential.

The positioning of the plants is important. It is extremely difficult to establish a large plant in a crevice which continually runs short of water although, in the wild, many species may seed themselves in positions which normally would be considered impossible for healthy growth. The root system on a seedling is proportional in size to the top growth and this may possibly occupy only a fraction of the room that the adult plant will finally require. The roots thus have an opportunity to spread out into all the little pockets and crevices, before the apparent space becomes occupied. This set of circumstances is therefore totally different from trying to establish the same size of plant in its mature form.

The addition of peat or similar organic material is beneficial to the plants. Whereas the dwarf and alpine species of rhododendrons are adapted to withstand extremes of sun and wind, conditions which are found in many of their native habitats, a measure of shelter from the worst of the drying winds will unquestionably aid their early establishment.

CHOICE OF SPECIES AND HYBRIDS

Within certain constraints, the choice of rhododendron for the rock garden depends largely on personal preference. In the majority of cases, a species or hybrid which would exceed 1.5 m in height, would be an unlikely choice, for large plants quickly smother or shade their smaller neighbours. Ideally, a wide range of species and cultivars, which will provide a continuity of flower through the early spring and into the summer months, should be chosen. This is more difficult to achieve in the rock garden, where smaller species are required, than in the woodland garden, where the later-flowering types can be used.

The size of the rock garden will determine the quantity planted, and although massed plantings may be successful in the larger botanic gardens, in the smaller garden it is probably better to grow as wide a range of species as possible. It is important to label those plants which can be positively identified and, at the same time, to keep a master record of their exact positions, in case the labels are moved or lost. This may seem laborious at first, but as enthusiasm grows the value of such an exercise will become apparent.

A list of suitable species and hybrids can be found in Appendix 1.

Appendix 3
Plant Associations

Size of Plants

It is perhaps somewhat arbitrary to group the various species, varieties and cultivars according to size, as size depends very much on the prevailing growing conditions. Some species, e.g. the so-called 'dwarf' conifers, may eventually grow much larger than anticipated whereas other species, generally seen as large specimens, may not attain their full size. There is an overlap between the size groups and you should not be afraid to experiment.

Common Names

Botanical names should be used whenever possible when ordering plants. Common names vary from country to country and even from locality to locality. Also, they frequently apply to more than one species.

Ordering Plants

Consult a good catalogue or book, e.g. *Hillier's Manual of Trees and Shrubs,* check the description, assess the suitability and, using the botanical name, order the plants. If in doubt, check with a reputable nurseryman, garden centre, botanical garden or local authority parks department.

Size of Garden

The concept of small, medium and large gardens is rather subjective. For the purpose of this book, 'small' refers to gardens up to 800 m², 'medium' to gardens of 800–8000 m² and 'large' to gardens of over 8000 m².

Soil Requirements

Rhododendrons belong to the Ericaceae and, in common with other members of this family, exhibit a preference for low pH soils. The soil in the garden, therefore, should generally be of a low pH. There are a wide range of acid-loving or acid-tolerant plants which can be grown in association with *Rhododendron,* e.g. *Erica, Calluna, Pernettya, Pieris.*

Apart from these members of the Ericaceae, genera such as *Lilium, Primula, Betula, Magnolia and Camellia* will also do well.

To increase the range of plants which can be grown, pockets of soil within the garden can be made alkaline by the addition of lime.

Planning the Garden

There are two approaches to garden planning. The person whose prime interest is the plants will probably have few preconceived ideas about their positioning. The person whose main concern is the garden as a whole will plan and organise each square metre of ground in order to make the maximum use of available space and will position the plants to contrast with, and to complement, each other. A compromise is probably the best course.

It is important when planting a species, *Rhododendron* or otherwise, to visualise the final height and diameter and, unless you are prepared to carry out a considerable amount of transplanting, room must be left for the plant to develop. Consider also the overall density of the plant, the amount of pruning which will be required to prevent the plant from overcrowding its neighbours, and even the damage which might result from large trunks or branches falling in a storm.

Choice of trees should be governed by the size of the garden and the size of the rhododendrons to be grown. The forest type of tree, e.g. oak or beech, should be confined to the large woodland garden where the larger species of *Rhododendron*, e.g. *R. sinogrande,* will be able to compete and to benefit from the resulting leafmould. Such trees are not recommended for small gardens, unless used as windbreaks or coppiced, for not only will their shade be too dense but their roots can undermine the foundations of buildings. The birch, however, which is of slender habit, will associate well with all but the smallest species and will suit a small garden. The shelter afforded by the trees should also be considered; e.g. a strategically placed conifer may provide just the right amount of shelter to protect a plant with opening flower buds from the early morning sun until the ambient temperature rises.

Ground Cover Suitable for All Gardens

This list is only a rough guide to the many species suitable for planting with rhododendrons. The main aim should be permanence so that the roots of the rhododendrons are not disturbed by annual lifting of the bulbs.

Anemone blanda (anemone, windflower)
Anemone nemorosa
Cardiocrinum giganteum (giant lily)
Chionodoxa spp. (glory of the snow)
Colchicum autumnale et al. (autumn crocus)
Crinum spp. (crinum)
Crocus (crocus) Most spp.
Cyclamen europaeum (cyclamen)
Cyclamen neapolitanum (cyclamen)
Erythronium (dog's tooth violet) Most spp.
Fritillaria (crown imperial, snake's head) Most spp.
Galanthus (snowdrop) Most spp.
Galtonia candicans (summer-flowering hyacinth)
Hyacinthus cvs. (hyacinth)
Iris danfordiae
Iris reticulata (iris)
Leucojum spp. (snowflake)
Lilium (lily) Most spp.
Muscari spp. (grape hyacinth)
Narcissus (narcissus, daffodil) Especially the dwarf spp.
Nerine bowdenii (nerine)
Ornithogalum spp. (star of Bethlehem)
Pulsatilla vulgaris (pasque flower)
Scilla (scilla) Most spp.

HERBACEOUS PERENNIALS INCLUDING ALPINES

Although a few of the larger-growing herbaceous perennials have been included, these are not so invasive as to swamp the smaller rhododendron species. This list is only an indication of the wide variety of species which will associate well with rhododendrons.

Ajuga (bugle) Spp. and cvs.
Androsace (rock jasmine) Many spp.
Calceolaria darwinii ⎫
Calceolaria tenella ⎭ (calceolaria)
Campanula (bell flower) Many spp.
Celmisia Many spp.
Cortaderia pumila ⎫
Cortaderia 'Sunningdale Silver' ⎭ (pampas grass)

Delphinium tatsienense (delphinium)
Euphorbia griffithii (euphorbia)
Festuca ovina (fescue)
Gentiana (gentian) Many spp. and cvs.
Helianthemum (rock rose) Many spp. and cvs.
Hosta (plantain lily) Most spp.
Incarvillea mairei (incarvillea)
Lysichitum americanum (American skunk cabbage)
Meconopsis betonicifolia ⎫
Meconopsis grandis ⎬ (Himalayan blue poppy)
Primula (primula) Most spp.
Trollius acaulis (globe flower)

Trees and Shrubs (Excluding Conifers)

FOR THE SMALL GARDEN

T = possibly tender in some areas or exposures.
  Acer griseum (maple)
  Acer palmatum vars, cvs. (Japanese maple)
  Acer pseudoplatanus 'Brilliantissimum'
  Andromeda spp. (bog rosemary)
T *Arbutus unedo* (strawberry tree)
  Artemisia spp. (southernwood)
  Arundinaria nitida (bamboo)
  Berberis (barberry) Many spp. and cvs. with exception of the larger
    ones.
  Betula (birch) Many spp. but on the border of being too large.
T *Callistemon salignus* (bottle brush)
  Calluna vulgaris (heather) Virtually all cvs.
T *Camellia* (camellia) Many spp. and cvs. will eventually grow quite large
    or will not always flower well. x *williamsii* is probably the best hybrid
    group.
  Caragana arborescens (pea tree)
T *Carpentaria californica* (carpentaria)
  Carpinus betulus 'Columnaris' (hornbeam)
  Cassiope (cassiope) Most spp. and cvs.
T *Ceanothus* (Californian lilac) Most spp. and cvs.
  Chaenomeles (quince) Most spp. and cvs.
  Chimonanthus praecox (winter sweet)

T *Choisya ternata* (Mexican orange blossom)
Cistus (rock or sun rose) Most spp.
Clematis (clematis) Especially *macropetala, montana* and *tangutica.*
Colutea arborescens (bladder senna)
Cordyline australis (New Zealand cabbage)
Cornus alba ⎫
Cornus kousa ⎬(dogwood)
T *Corylopsis* (corylopsis) Most spp.
Cotinus coggyria (smoke tree)
Cotoneaster (cotoneaster) Many spp. but a few cvs. such as 'Cornubia' can grow too large.
Crinodendron (*Tricuspidaria*) *hookerianum* (Chilean lantern tree)
Cytisus (broom) Most spp. and cvs.
Daboecia cantabrica cvs. (Irish heath)
Daphne (daphne) Most spp.
T *Desfontainea spinosa* (desfontainea)
Disanthus cercidifolius (disanthus)
T *Drimys winteri* (winter bark)
Dryas octopetala (mountain avens)
Eleagnus pungens 'Variegata' (eleagnus)
T *Embothrium lanceolatum* (Chilean fire bush)
Enkianthus campanulatus (enkianthus)
Erica (heath) Virtually all spp. and cvs., including tree-types.
Escallonia (escallonia) Many spp. and cvs. but avoid large-growing types.
T *Eucalyptus* (gum tree) Many spp. but will definitely grow too large. Worth replacing every 5–6 years.
T *Eucryphia* (eucryphia) Many spp. but could eventually grow too large for a small garden.
Euonymus fortunei radicans cvs. (evergreen spindle bush)
Forsythia 'Lynwood' (golden bell bush)
Fothergilla monticola (fothergilla)
Fuchsia magellanica (fuchsia)
Garrya elliptica (garrya) Good on walls. Could grow slightly too large.
Genista (broom, gorse) Most spp. and cvs.
Gleditsia triacanthos 'Elegantissima' (honey locust)
T *Griselinia littoralis* 'Variegata' (griselinia)
Hamamelis (witch hazel) Many spp. and cvs.
Hebe (hebe, erroneously called veronica) Most spp. and cvs.
Hibiscus syriacus (mallow)

Hydrangea (hydrangea) Spp. and cvs.

Hypericum (loosely named St John's wort and rose of Sharon) Many
    spp. and cvs.

Jasminium nudiflorum (jasmine) For walls.

Kalmia latifolia (calico bush)

Laurus nobilis (bay laurel)

Lavandula spica (lavender)

Ledum groenlandicum (Labrador tea plant)

T *Leptospermum scoparium* (tea tree)

Leycesteria formosa (flowering nutmeg)

Liquidambar styraciflua (sweet gum)

T *Lithospermum diffusum* (lithospermum)

Magnolia kobus
Magnolia x *soulangiana* } (magnolia) Best on walls.
Magnolia stellata

Mahonia aquifoliam
Mahonia bealei } (Oregon grape)

Malus sargentii
Malus tschonoskii } (flowering crabs)

Menziesia spp.

Myrtus apiculata (*luma*) (myrtle)

T *Olearia* (daisy bush) Many spp.

Osmanthus delavayi (osmanthus)

Osmanthus x *Osmarea* 'Burkwoodii' (osmarea)

Pachysandra terminalis 'Variegata' (pachysandra)

Paeonia lutea
Paeonia suffruticosa } (tree peony)

Philadelphus (mock orange) Perhaps 'Virginal'.

Philesia magellanica (philesia)

Phormium colensoi (New Zealand flax) *P. tenax* could grow too large.

Phyllodoce spp. (phyllodoce)

Pieris spp. (pieris) Can grow rather large.

Pittosporum (pittosporum) Most spp.

Potentilla (shrubby cinquefoil) Most spp.

Prunus x *blireana*
Prunus cerasifera
Prunus serrula } (flowering cherries)
Prunus subhirtella 'Autumnalis'

Pyracantha spp. (firethorn)

Pyrus salicifolia 'Pendula' (willow-leaved pear)

Rhus typhina (stag's horn sumach)
Ribes sanguineum (flowering currant)
Robinia pseudoacacia 'Frisia' (false acacia, black locust)
Rosa (rose) Shrubby spp. only, particularly 'Canary Bird', *moyesii*, *omeiensis* var. *pteracantha*.
Salix alba 'Chermesina' ('Britzensis') (scarlet willow)
Santolina chamaecyparissus (*incana*) (lavender cotton)
Senecio greyi (senecio)
Skimmia spp. (skimmia)

Sorbus aucuparia
Sorbus commixta
Sorbus hupehensis
Sorbus 'Joseph Rock' } (rowan, mountain ash)
Sorbus scalaris
Sorbus vilmorinii

Spiraea spp. (spiraea)
Stachyurus chinensis (stachyurus)
Vaccinium
Viburnum Most spp.
Yucca (Adam's needle) Many spp. but commonly *filamentosa* and *gloriosa*.

FOR THE MEDIUM-SIZED GARDEN

The trees and shrubs mentioned in the previous section would all be suitable for the medium-sized garden. Those listed below are additional.

Acer (maples) All spp. and cvs. except *pseudoplatanus* and possibly *platanoides*.
Aesculus x *carnea* 'Briotii' (red horse chestnut)
Ailanthus altissima (tree of heaven)
Ameliancher (snowy mespilus) Most spp.
Aralia spp. (Chinese angelica tree, devils walking)
Betula spp. (birch)
Buddleia (butterfly bush) Virtually all spp. and cvs.
Carpinus betulus (hornbeam) Cvs. and some spp. but not the type sp.
Castanea (chestnut) All spp. except *sativa*.
Cercidiphyllum japonicum (cercidiphyllum)
Cotoneaster (cotoneaster) All larger spp. and cvs.
Crataegus (hawthorn, quickthorn, etc.) All spp.
Davidia involucrata (pocket-handkerchief tree)

Fagus sylvatica (beech) Cvs. but not type sp.

Fraxinus excelsior (common ash) Cvs. but not type sp., *ornus* and some others.

Hoheria spp. (hoheria)

Ilex (holly) Spp. and cvs. but in moderation.

Magnolia (magnolia) All spp. but select site depending on size.

Morus spp. (mulberry) Possibly.

Nothofagus spp. (southern beeches)

Photinia spp. (photinia)

Populus (poplar) Some spp. but not *nigra*.

Prunus (flowering cherries) Most spp.

Quercus (oak) Smaller spp. only. Not often available.

Robinia spp. (false acacia, black locust)

Salix spp., cvs. (willow)

Sambucus spp., cvs. (elder)

Sorbus spp. (whitebeams, rowans)

Stranvaesia davidiana (stranvaesia) And cvs.

Syringa (lilac) Possibly.

Tilia (lime) But not x *europa* or *platyphyllos*, type hybrid or type sp.

Ulmus (elms) Only smaller-growing spp. and cvs. if available, e.g. x *sarniensis* 'Dicksonii'.

FOR THE LARGE GARDEN

These include all the large-growing forest-type trees, species which would normally be too large or too dense for the smaller garden. They should be planted well away from buildings because of the danger of falling branches, the effects of their roots on the foundations and the shade which they afford.

Conifers

FOR THE SMALL GARDEN

Abies koreana (fir)

Chaemaecyparis lawsoniana 'Nana' (Lawson cypress)

Chamaecyparis obtusa (Hinoki cypress) Many dwarf-growing cvs. in green and gold.

Chamaecyparis pisifera (Sawara cypress) Many dwarf- and small-growing cvs.

Cryptomeria japonica (Japanese cedar) Several dwarf- and small-growing cvs.

Cupressus macrocarpa (Monterey cypress) Several dwarf- and small-growing forms.

Gingko biloba (maidenhair tree) Will grow fairly tall but does not generally spread.

Juniperus (juniper) Many spp. and cvs. of dwarf, medium-sized and ground cover plants in greens, golds and blues.

Picea abies (Norway spruce — type sp.) Many cvs. in every size, shape and colour.

Picea pungens (Colorado spruce) As above.

Pinus patula (pine) Could eventually grow too large.

Pinus pumila (dwarf Siberian pine)

Pinus sylvestris (Scots pine — type sp.) Several slow-growing cvs.

Sequoia sempervirens 'Adpressa' (Californian redwood — type sp.) Can revert to large type of tree.

Taxus baccata (common yew) Several slow-growing and highly decorative cultivars.

Thuja occidentalis (American arbor-vitae — type sp.) Many slow-growing ornamental cvs.

Thuja orientalis (Chinese arbor-vitae — type sp.) As above.

Thuja plicata (Western red cedar — type sp.) As above.

Tsuga canadensis (Eastern hemlock — type sp.) As above.

FOR MEDIUM-SIZED AND LARGE GARDENS

In addition to those listed below, the forest-type species can be planted in large gardens.

Cedrus atlantica glauca
Cedrus deodara 'Pendula'
Cedrus libani } (cedars) Although these may grow too large for the medium-sized garden this should not happen for years.

Chamaecyparis lawsoniana (cypress) The larger cvs. are probably not suitable unless pruning, hedging or eventual removal is contemplated.

Cryptomeria japonica 'Elegans' (Japanese cedar) This will eventually grow fairly large.

Cupressocyparis leylandii (Leyland cypress) Can be used as a hedge or windbreak. Without trimming it will attain enormous height. 'Castwellan' is slower-growing.

Cupressus (cyprus) Larger-growing cvs.

Picea brewerana (Brewer's weeping spruce) Will eventually grow fairly
   large.
Picea pungens glauca
Picea pungens 'Koster' }(blue spruce) As above.
Thujopsis dolobrata (thujopsis) Type and cvs. will eventually grow
   fairly large.

Appendix 4
Windbreaks

Many materials, both natural and man-made, can be used as windbreaks and it is worth experimenting with locally available products to determine their suitability.

Manufactured Materials

HESSIAN

Hessian and similar fabrics made from natural fibres have been available for hundreds of years. Currently it is losing favour to many of the man-made fibres but nevertheless it still has its uses. It can be excellent for short-term work, especially where individual plants need to be protected from wind, snow or frost, but strong supports are essential. Also it can be purchased in several widths and qualities.

Its disadvantages lie in its price and its durability, especially in regions of high rainfall. Most types of hessian tend to be too dense for the theoretically correct semi-permeable windbreak.

POLYPROPYLENE MESH

Polypropylene mesh has many uses in horticulture not the least of which is protection from wind damage. The material is available in various widths and mesh sizes, is long lasting and relatively cheap. Green, which is the most popular colour, blends well into the background. As with hessian, strong supports are necessary to prevent the mesh from being blown away.

CHAIN-LINK AND WELDED MESH FENCING

While both of these material are long-lasting and can be utilised, with some additional material, to provide a fairly substantial windbreak, they are too expensive to use for this purpose alone. If, however, it is intended to provide a fence around the property anyway then the extra cost may be justified. Tensioning wires and strong supports are essential.

CHICKEN- AND RABBIT-FENCING

Chicken- or rabbit-wire mesh is quite commonly used to provide protection from rabbits or deer but can be used quite effectively for wind protection, providing that other materials, such as dried bracken, are added to increase the density. The mesh is available in different widths.

CHESPALE FENCING

Chespale fencing is extensively used by parks and similar departments to provide a barrier to pedestrians. Providing that the fence is well supported, chespale can be effective as a windbreak; in some situations, however, the density may have to be increased. The principal advantage is that it should last for many years.

BAMBOO MATTING

Bamboo matting was once commonly used on framelights to provide frost protection during very cold weather. Unfortunately it did not stand up to rough handling and consequently had to be replaced at frequent intervals. However, a low-density bamboo screen can be very effective against wind and, where there is a ready source of this plant, it is a relatively simple task to tie the cut canes to a horizontal support, thus providing a cheap and long-lasting windbreak.

WEBBING

Within the last few years, plastic webbing has found favour with many of the large commercial nurseries and garden centres. This material offers many advantages, such as long life, great strength, ease of handling. Although it is not particularly cheap it is well worth considering.

Suitable Trees and Shrubs

The following species make excellent windbreaks because of their dense growth and their hardiness.

TREES

Abies lasiocarpa
Abies pinsapo } (silver fir)
Abies procera
Acer pseudoplatanus (sycamore)

Cupressus macrocarpa (Monterey cypress)
Fagus sylvatica (beech)
Larix decidua (larch)
Pinus contorta (beach pine)
Pinus nigra var. *maritima* (Corsican pine)
Quercus ilex (holm oak)
Quercus robur (common oak)
Salix spp. (willow)
Sorbus aria (whitebeam)
Sorbus aucuparia (mountain ash, rowan)

SHRUBS

Arundinaria Many spp. but avoid those which spread too rapidly unless there is sufficient room.
Escallonia Especially 'Langleyensis'
Griselinia littoralis
Hippophae rhamnoides (sea buckthorn)
Olearia x *haastii*
Olearia traversii } (daisy bushes) More suitable for coastal regions.
Rhododendron ponticum Can get out of control.
Sambucus nigra (common elder)

Appendix 5
Generally Available Fertilisers and Their Suitability for Rhododendrons

Name of fertiliser	Constituent	Approximate % of constituent	Recommended	Application rate
Iron-based				
chelated iron	Fe		Yes	To soil: 120–150 g in 30 l water/10 m² To foliage: 30 g/100 l water
ferrous sulphate	FeSO₄		Yes	3 kg/10 m²
Magnesium-based				
Epsom salts	MgO	17	Yes	1 kg/20 m²
Nitrogen-based				
ammonium nitrate	N	35	No	
ammonium sulphate	N + S	21	Yes	68 g/m²
calcium nitrate	N + Ca	15.5	No	
Chilean nitrate of potash	N + K₂O	15 + 10	No	
gold N	N	36	Yes. Early in the year	15–30 g/m²
mono-ammonium phosphate	N + P	12	Yes	15 g/m²
nitro-chalk	N + Ca	21	No	
sodium nitrate	N + Na	16	No	
urea	N	46.5	Yes	15–30 g/m²
cow manure (well rotted)	N	0.15	Yes (as mulch)	25–50 mm deep
dried blood	N	11–13		
hoof and horn meal	N	11–13	Yes	30 g/m²

Name of fertiliser	Constituent	Approximate % of constituent	Recommended	Application rate
Phosphorus-based				
basic slag	$P_2O_5 + Ca$	7–22	No	
bone flour	$P_2O_5N + Ca$	28	⎫ In high rain-	⎫
bone meal	$P_2O_5N + Ca$	22 + 4	⎬ fall areas	⎬ 15 g/m²
meat and bonemeal	$P_2O_5N + Ca$	20 + 6	⎭ only	⎭
ground mineral phosphates	P_2O_5	25–40	Yes	15–30 g/m²
mono-ammonium phosphate	P_2O_5	60	Yes	15 g/m²
triple superphosphate	P_2O_5	47	Yes	15–30 g/m²
superphosphate	P_2O_5	18.5	Yes. In small quantities unless soil is of low pH	122 g/m²
Potassium-based				
Chilean nitrate of potash	$K_2O + N$	10 + 15	No	
magnesium potassium phosphate	$K_2O + Mg + P_2O_5$	7	No data available but almost certainly no adverse effects	60 g/m²
muriate of potash	K_2O	60	No data	
potassium nitrate	$K_2O + N$	46.4	No	
potassium sulphate	$K_2O + S$	50	Yes	50 g/m²
Compound Fertilisers				
Enmag	⎫		⎫	
John Innes Base	⎪		⎪	
Osmocote	⎬ See manufacturer's data sheets		⎬ Yes	
Plantasan	⎪		⎪	
Vitax	⎭		⎭	
Trace Elements				
fritted trace elements 253A	See manufacturer's data sheet		Yes	390 g/m³

Appendix 6
Specialist Societies

Wherever the genus *Rhododendron* can be grown with any degree of success, enthusiastic groups have been formed to exchange information, plants and knowledge, and spread interest in what is probably the most prolific genus cultivated by man. The societies listed below have provided information about their activities.

Australia

THE AUSTRALIAN RHODODENDRON SOCIETY

The Society issues a quarterly journal, *The Rhododendron,* in which there are articles, by growers, fanciers and collectors, on the best and most up-to-date information available on rhododendrons in Australia, including both deciduous and evergreen azaleas and the semi-tropical Malesian group of rhododendrons. The Society year commences on 1 July and members who join during the year are entitled to back numbers of publications for that year. Membership fees are fixed on the basis of family membership for husband and wife, who receive one copy of all publications.

The Society has branches in Victoria, Tasmania, South Australia and Illawarra. Further enquiries should be addressed to Mr J. Clyde Smith, 15 Cassian Street, Keiraville, N.S.W. 2500, Australia.

British Isles

THE RHODODENDRON AND CAMELLIA GROUP

The Rhododendron and Camellia Group was re-constituted in 1976 under a committee, after being run from Wisley for 30 years. Organised interest in the cultivation of rhododendrons in the United Kingdom dates from 1915, with the formation of the Rhododendron Society, of which the first Honorary Secretary was Mr Charles Eley.

The Rhododendron Society, with only 25 members, merged, in 1931, with the much larger Rhododendron Association, which had been formed in 1929 under the presidency of Mr Lionel de Rothschild. In 1939, the Association had 477 members, but, with the outbreak of war, it was taken over by the Royal Horticultural Society and, in 1946, the Rhododendron Group was formed. This, in 1954, became the Rhododendron and Camellia Group.

The group publishes the internationally famous yearbook which has undergone several name changes but is now called *Rhododendrons with Magnolias and Camellias*. This is supplemented by the bulletin which is produced quarterly. The parent body — The Royal Horticultural Society — also prints many leaflets and handbooks with sections containing information on the cultivation of a wide range of shrubs, including rhododendrons. The Group holds various competitions and shows, the largest of which takes place in the R.H.S. New Hall during March, April or early May.

Annual visits to rhododendron gardens in various regions of the British Isles are a feature of the group's activities. The purchase of specialist literature is often made available through the pages of the bulletin and correspondence on topics of interest are actively encouraged. Further enquiries to Mr J. Waugh Owens, Honorary Secretary, The Rhododendron and Camellia Group, Jubilee Lodge, Yarpole, Leominster, Herefordshire HR6 OBA.

Canada

RHODODENDRON SOCIETY OF CANADA

The Society was founded in 1971 and is dedicated to the propagation, cultivation and enjoyment of the genus *Rhododendron,* and to the stimulation of interest in rhododendrons and azaleas among home and landscape gardeners, nurserymen, garden centres, other retailers and the general public.

Membership is invited from home gardeners, individuals and families, horticultural societies, garden clubs and institutional organisations. The Society provides illustrated presentations to interested groups, has regular meetings for members and arranges garden tours, as well as publishing a twice-yearly illustrated bulletin. In addition, the Society holds auction sales, maintains a library of colour slides, films and books and operates a seed exchange scheme.

Regional groups have been formed in the Atlantic, Niagara Peninsula and Toronto areas. Further enquiries should be addressed to The Rhododendron Society of Canada, 2151 Camilla Road, Mississauga, Ontario L5A 2K1, Canada.

Japan

THE JAPANESE RHODODENDRON SOCIETY

The Japanese Rhododendron Society publishes a quarterly journal (written in Japanese), maintains a plant and pollen bank, and operates a seed exchange scheme and a photographic library. In addition to flower shows, a national convention is held every other year.

There are 29 chapters located throughout the country. Further enquiries should be addressed to The Japanese Rhododendron Society, c/o Mr Hideo Ohshima, 2-19-16 Harigaya, Urawa-shi, Saitama-Ken 338, Japan.

New Zealand

DUNEDIN RHODODENDRON GROUP

The group issues an annual journal which contains colour plates and articles from enthusiasts, both amateur and professional, throughout the world. Some of the facilities offered by the group include lectures approximately 6 times per year, plant sales, newsletters, and visits to interesting gardens. Further enquiries should be addressed to Mr S. J. Grant, Secretary, Dunedin Rhododendron Group, 25 Pollock Street, Maori Hill, Dunedin.

THE NEW ZEALAND RHODODENDRON ASSOCIATION

The Association was founded in 1944 to encourage the cultivation, study and improvement of rhododendrons, and to act as a common meeting ground for enthusiasts.

The Association publishes bulletins at frequent intervals, distributes new species and cultivars, and organises lectures and visits to gardens of interest. In 1969, the Association acquired ground at Kimbolton, where an extensive collection of plant material is being built up. Further enquiries to The Secretary, The New Zealand Rhododendron Association, P.O. Box 28, Palmerston North, New Zealand.

United States of America

THE AMERICAN RHODODENDRON SOCIETY

Among the services provided to members of the Society are: a seventy-page quarterly bulletin in colour, containing articles by growers, fanciers and collectors; an extensive list of rhododendron seeds which are available at minimal cost; other publications relating to rhododendrons and azaleas at nominal cost. Chapter affiliation, included in the annual membership fee, offers additional advantages in the form of various activities. Most provide monthly informative meetings, newsletters, garden tours, study groups, plant auctions and flower shows. Many chapters maintain display gardens for the enjoyment of the community.

There are 38 chapters all over the United States of America, one in Vancouver, Canada, and another in Denmark. Further enquiries should be addressed to Mrs E. D. Egan, 14635 SW Bull Mt Read, Tigard OR 97223, U.S.A.

THE PACIFIC RHODODENDRON SOCIETY

The Society provides, in addition to their monthly newsletters, a considerable amount of literature, either free or at a relatively small cost. Other activities include monthly meetings, annual landscape show, plant sales and visits to famous and interesting gardens.

There are 3 chapters situated in Washington State. Further enquiries should be addressed to Marlene Buffington, Executive Secretary, 1202 Sunset Drive, Tacoma, Washington 98465, U.S.A.

THE RHODODENDRON SPECIES FOUNDATION

The Species Foundation was started in the 1960s by a small group of enthusiasts, when they acquired a 23-acre site from the Weyerhaeuser Company. The garden has been designed on a geographical basis to show representative collections of species from China, Tibet, Nepal, Sikkim, Assam, Bhutan, Burma, Japan, Korea, etc.

The following facilities are offered to members: a quarterly newsletter, photographs and other publications at a small cost, plant distribution lists. The Foundation has also begun a correspondence course entitled *Introduction to the Study of Species Rhododendron*. This course should prove extremely valuable to the beginner and experienced grower who has perhaps studied only hybrids in the past. Further information is available from Karen S. Gunderson, Administrator, P.O. Box 3798, Federal Way WA 98003, Washington, U.S.A.

146

This, like many other Societies, distributes various publications on the subject, holds annual shows, meetings, etc. Further enquiries to The Washington Rhododendron Society, Box 132, Puyallup, Washington, U.S.A.

Appendix 7
Gardens Open Regularly to the Public

The main problem in providing a list of interesting or worthwhile gardens to visit is the variation in standard which occurs in the lifespan of any one garden. Apart from abnormal weather conditions, finance, matters of ownership and politics may all play their part in the welfare of a garden. Moreover, it is obviously impossible to visit every garden possessing a collection of rhododendrons in order to assess it personally.

The lists of gardens in the British Isles have been compiled with the help of many bodies, notably the National Gardens Schemes. In addition to those gardens owned by the National Trust, Department of Agriculture and the Royal Horticultural Society, many private gardens not listed in the publications of the Garden Schemes are also open throughout the year. The various specialist rhododendron societies throughout the world (see Appendix 6) have provided information on gardens elsewhere.

The criterion which I have used for including a garden is that it must contain a representative collection of rhododendrons, either planted in a particularly interesting way, or of historical importance and well labelled or otherwise recorded. Certain excellent gardens in the British Isles, which come under the Gardens Schemes, have been omitted as they are open only on certain days of the year. So have many other gardens which contain large numbers of the genus but have a significant amount of duplication with very little variation. This is often the case where the rhododendron has been used for its landscaping effect alone. Many gardens not listed are well worth visiting and reference to an appropriate booklet is recommended before a visit (see Appendix 9). Other gardens have been included because, although to the non-plantsman they might look unkempt, at least the plants are thriving to such an extent that regeneration is taking place.

Australia

The Australian Rhododendron Society have indicated that a complete list is not yet available as interest in the genus is relatively new in their country.

The National Rhododendron Garden, Olinda, Australia.

British Isles

NT – National Trust; *NGS* – National Garden Scheme

ENGLAND

Berkshire
Saville Gardens, Windsor Crown Estate   March–Dec.

Cheshire
Tatton Park, Knutsford *NT*   All year

Cornwall
Antony House, Torpoint *NT*   March–Oct.
Cothele, Calstock *NT NGS*   March–Oct.
Glendurgan, Falmouth *NT*   March–Oct.
Lanhydrock, Bodmin *NT*   March–Oct.
Pencarrow House, Bodmin *Private*   March–Sept.
Trewithen, Probus *Private*
Trengwainton, Penzance *NT NGS*   March–Oct.
Trelissick, Truro *NT NGS*   March–Oct.

Cumbria
Stagshaw, Ambleside *NT NGS*
Holker Hall, Grange-over-Sands *Private NGS*   April–Sept. (except Saturdays)
Holehird, Troutbeck, *Lake District Horticultural Society*

Devon
Arlington Court, Barnstaple *NT*   March–Oct.
Castle Drogo, Drewsteignton *NT NGS*
The Garden House, Yelverton *Private* April–Sept. (every Wednesday)
Killerton, Exeter *NT NGS*
Knightshayes Court, Tiverton *NT NGS*
Saltram, Plympton *NT NGS*

Dorset
Compton Acres, Poole *Private NGS*   April–Oct.
Minterne, Cerne Abbas *Private NGS*   April–June (mainly Sundays)

Gloucestershire
Abbotswood, Stow-on-the-Wold *Private NGS*

Hampshire
Exbury, Beaulieu *Private NGS*   April–June

Herefordshire
Herrington Hall, Leominster *NT*   April–Sept.
Hergest Croft, Hereford *Private NGS*   May–Oct.

Kent
Emmetts Garden, Ide Hill *NT*   April, July–Oct.
The Grange, Benenden *Private NGS*
Hole Park, Rolvendeon *Private NGS*
Ladham House, Goudhurst *Private NGS*
The Old Vicarage, Ide Hill *Private NGS*
Oxon Heath, Hadlow *Private NGS*
The Red House, Crockham Hill *Private NGS*
Sandling Park, Hythe *Private NGS*
Scotney Castle, Lamberhurst *NT*   March–Oct.
Stonewall Park, Chiddingstone Heath *Private NGS*
Tanners, Brasted *Private NGS*

Merseyside
Ness Botanic Gardens, Liverpool *University of Liverpool*

Greater Manchester
Dunham, Massey *NT*
Lyme Park, Stockport *NT*   March–Oct.

Norfolk
Blicking Hall, Aylsham *NT NGS*   March–Oct.
Felbrigg Hall, Cromer *NT NGS*   March–Oct.

Northumberland
Cragside, Rothbury *NT NGS*   March–Sept.

Nottinghamshire
Clumber Park, Worksop *NT NGS*   All year

Salop
Dudmaston, Bridgnorth *NT NGS*

Staffordshire and West Midlands
Shugborough, Stafford *NT NGS* March–Oct.
Wightwick Manor, Wolverhampton *NT NGS* All year

Surrey
Grayswood Hill, Haslemere *Private NGS*
Kew, The Royal Botanic Gardens *Ministry of Agriculture, Fisheries and Food*
Leith Hill Place, Dorking *NT*
Winkworth Arboretum, Godalming *NT NGS*

Sussex (East and West)
Borde Hill Garden, Haywards Heath *NGS* March–Sept.
Heaselands, Haywards Heath *Private NGS*
High Beeches, Hand Cross *Private NGS*
Malt House, Chithurst, Rogate *Private NGS*
Nymans Gardens, Hand Cross *NT NGS* March–Oct.
Petworth House, Petworth *NT* March–Oct.
Sheffield Park Garden, Uckfield *NT* March–Sept.
Standen, East Grinstead *NT* March–Oct.
Wakehurst Place, Haywards Heath *NT* All year

Wiltshire
Stourhead, Mere *NT NGS* All year

WALES

Clwyd
Chirk Castle, Wrexham *NT*

Dyfed
Dolby Lodge, Amroth *NT NGS*

Gwynedd
Bodnant, Talycafin, Colwyn Bay *NT* March–Oct.

Gwent
Yew Tree, Lydart *Private NGS*

Powys
Powis Castle, Welshpool *NT NGS* May–Sept.

* Particularly good. *SGS* See Scotland's Garden Scheme booklet. *NTS* National Trust for Scotland

Argyll and Bute District Council
*Achamore House, Gigha *Private SGS* April–Oct.
Achnacloich, Connel *Private SGS* April–June
Ardanaiseig, Kilchrennan *Private SGS* April–Oct.
*Arduaine, Kilmelford *Private* All year (except Thursdays)
*Crarae Gardens, Minard *Private SGS* All year
Kilmory Castle, Lochgilphead *Argyll and Bute District Council* All year
Stonefield Castle, Tarbert *Private* All year
Strone, Cairndow *Private SGS* April–Sept.
*Younger Botanic Gardens, Dunoon *Department of Agriculture and Fisheries SGS* April–Oct.

Cunninghame District Council
*Brodick Castle, Brodick (Arran) *NTS SGS* All year (gardens only)

Dumbarton District Council
Glenarn, Rhu *Private SGS* Temporarily closed

Edinburgh City District Council
*Royal Botanic Gardens, Edinburgh *Department of Agriculture and Fisheries* All year

Glasgow City District Council
Pollok House, Glasgow *Glasgow District Council* All year

Inverclyde and Renfrew District Councils
Finlaystone House, Langbank *Private SGS* All year

Kyle and Carrick District Council
Bargany, Girvan *Private SGS* Feb.–Oct.
Culzean, Maybole *NTS SGS* All year

Perth and Kinross District Council
Branklyn, Perth *NTS SGS* March–Oct.
*Glendoick, Perth *Private SGS* All year (garden centre only)

Ross and Cromarty District Council
Inverewe, Poolewe *NTS SGS* All year

Stewartry District Council
Threave, Castle Douglas *NTS SGS*   All year

Stirling District Council
Gargunnock, Stirling *Private SGS*
Keir, Dunblane *Private SGS*   April–Oct.

Tweeddale District Council
Dawyck House, Stobo *Private SGS*
Dawyck Arboretum, Stobo *Department of Agriculture and Fisheries SGS*   All year

Wigtown District Council
Castle Kennedy Gardens, Stranraer *Private SGS*   April–Sept.
Galloway House Gardens, Garlieston *Private SGS*   May–Sept.
*Logan Botanic Gardens, Stranraer *Department of Agriculture and Fisheries SGS*   April–Sept.

NORTHERN IRELAND

Down
Ballyulolly *Private*
Ballywater House *Private*
Castle Ward, Downpatrick *NT*
Castlewellan, Castlewellan *Private*
Guincho Garden
Mount Stewart, Newtownards *NT*
Rowallane, Saintfield *NT*

Fermanagh
Florence Court, Enniskillen *NT*

REPUBLIC OF IRELAND (excluding National Trust Property)

Cork
Abbey Leix, Port Laoise *Private*
Annes Grove, Castletownroche *Private*
Bantry House, Bantry *Private*
Fota *Private*
Ilnacullin, Garanish Island *Private*

Donegal
Glenveagh, Loughveagh *Private*
Kildrum Gardens *Private*

Dublin
Glasnevin Botanic Gardens, Dublin *National*
Howth Castle, Dublin *Private*
Malahide Castle, Malahide *Private*

Kerry
Ch. Ardnagashield House, Glengariff *Private*
Derreen, Kilmackillogue Harbour *Private*
Muckross House, Killarney *Private*
Rossdohan, Parknasilla *Public Works*

Limerick
Adare Manor, Limerick *Private*

Offaly
Birr Castle, Birr *Private*

Waterford
Lismore Gardens, Lismore *Private*
Mount Congrieve, Waterford *Private*

Wexford
Johnstown Castle *Private*

Wicklow
Mount Usher, Ashford
Powerscourt, Enniskerry *Private*

Canada

BRITISH COLUMBIA

Burnaby Centennial Park, Canada Way, Burnaby. Hybrids.
Butchard Gardens, Victoria.
Minter Garden, P.O. Box 40, Chilliwack, BC V2P 6H7.
Park and Telford Gardens, North Vancouver. Hybrids. Very small planting as background for various formal and informal gardens.
Queen Elizabeth Park, Vancouver. Species and hybrids. Mostly new plantings adjacent to Bloedell Conservatory.
Stanley Park, Vancouver. Species and hybrids. Most plants in the general area of the Parks Board Offices.
University of British Columbia, Vancouver. Several sizeable and established plantings on the campus of species, hybrids and azaleas. Collection reasonably well documented and labelled but as yet does

not have display labels so difficult for general public to get information.

University of British Columbia Botanical Garden, 6501 NW Marine Drive, Vancouver, BC V6T 1W5. Collection totals about 300 different species and forms. Propagated vegetatively from specific plants of known origin in the British Isles, many from collectors of original plants. Collection not open for public viewing at the moment but interested individuals or groups may view the collection by appointment, by contacting the Office of the Botanical Garden.

University of Victoria Gardens, Victoria.

Van Dusen Gardens, Oak Street, Vancouver. Converted from a city golf course in the early seventies, this 55-acre site contains an extensive collection of the most recent rhododendron hybrids.

'The Glades', Surrey. A private garden open to the public from late April through May. Five acres of rhododendrons (mostly species), azaleas (many highly perfumed) and trees from all over the world grow side by side with the native trees. A photographer's paradise.

NOVA SCOTIA

Halifax Public Park, Halifax. Very old established plantings of both evergreen rhododendrons and deciduous azaleas. Large thickets of Mollis azaleas are especially vigorous.

Kentville Research Station, Kentville. Canada Department of Agriculture. Without question, the finest development of mature plantings of both species and hybrids in eastern Canada. Best weekend in June for seeing the plants in bloom is known as Rhododendron Sunday.

ONTARIO

Dominion Arboretum Agriculture Canada, Central Experimental Farm, Ottawa. Fairly large collection, chiefly of hybrids, planted in beds in a sheltered area of the arboretum. Newer cultivars are continually being assessed for their hardiness and added to the collection. Best time to visit is late May to early June.

Edwards Gardens, Toronto. Plantings of species and hybrid rhododendrons and azaleas, plus a small planting of mature plants in the valley of the garden.

Royal Botanical Gardens, Hamilton. Fairly large plantings of mainly hybrids situated behind the Nature Centre, plus various small plantings in the rockery.

Woodland Nurseries, Mississauga. Scattered evergreen plantings in 4 acres of woodland. Both species and hybrids of evergreen and deciduous rhododendrons. Best time to view the plants in bloom is the last week in May and first week in June.

Japan

Himenosawa Shizen Koen Shakunage En, 1164–1 Himenosawa, Izusan, Atami-shi, Shizuoka-Ken

Shuzenji Shizen Koen Shakunage No Mori, Cahibayama, Shuzenji, Shuzenji-cho, To Hoh-Gun, Shizuoka-Ken

Tsutsuji Ga-oka, Tatebayashi, Gumma-Ken

New Zealand

By courtesy of Dunedin Rhododendron Group and New Zealand Rhododendron Association.

SOUTH ISLAND

Dunedin Botanic Gardens, Opoha Road, Dunedin North
Glenfalloch Gardens, Portobello Road, RD2, Dunedin
Ilam Garden, University of Canterbury, Christchurch
Larnach Castle, Pukehiki, P.O. Box 1350, Dunedin
Queens Park, Queens Drive, Invercargill

NORTH ISLAND

New Zealand Rhododendron Association, Kimbolton (near Palmerston North)
Pukeiti Rhododendron Trust, New Plymouth
Pukekura Park, New Plymouth
Mr Eric Wilson's Garden and Nursery, Kimbolton (near Palmerston North)

United States of America

By courtesy of the American Rhododendron Society.

ALABAMA

Bellingarth Gardens, Theodore AL 36582 (John H. Brown 205–973–2217). Open 7 a.m.–dusk

Birmingham Botanical Gardens, 2612 Lane Park Road, Birmingham AL 35223 (Gary G. Gerlach, Director 205–879–1576)

CALIFORNIA

Descanso Gardens, Department of Arboreta and Botanic Gardens, 1418 Descanso Drive, LA Canada, CA 91011. Open 8 a.m.–5.30 p.m.

Golden Gate Park, San Francisco, CA 94117

Strybing Arboretum and Botanical Gardens, Golden Gate Park, 9th Avenue and Lincoln Way, San Francisco, CA 94122 (Tel: 415–558–3622)

University of California Botanical Garden, Strawberry Canyon, Berkeley, CA 94720 (Tel: 415–642–3343)

DELAWARE

Winterthur Gardens, Winterthur, DE 19735 (Tel: 302–656–8591)

DISTRICT OF COLUMBIA

U.S. National Arboretum, Washington, DC 20002 (Tel: 202–399–5400)

FLORIDA

Florida Cypress Gardens, Box 1, Cypress Gardens, FL 33880

GEORGIA

Callayay Gardens, Pine Mountain, GA 31822 (Fred C. Galle). Open 9 a.m.–5 p.m.

Fernbank Science Center, 156 Heaton Park Drive, Atlanta, GA 30307 (Tel: 404–378–4311)

University of Georgia Botanical Garden, Plant Sciences Building, University of Georgia, Athens, GA 30602 (Tel: 404–542–1244)

ILLINOIS

Chicago Horticultural Society and Botanic Garden, Room 600, 18 South Michigan Avenue, Chicago, IL 60603 (Tel: 312–332–2868)

KENTUCKY

Bernheim Forest Arboretum, Clermont, KY 40110 (Tel: 502–543–2451)

LOUISIANA

Gloster Arboretum, Box 1106, Baton Rouge, LA 70821 (Tel: 504-342-4447)

Live Oak Gardens, Jefferson Island, P.O. Box 284, New Iberia, LA 70560 (Tel: 318-365-3631)

Hodges Garden, Box 921, Many, LA 71449 (Tel: 586-3591)

University of South-western Louisiana, Ira S. Nelson Horticulture Center, Box 4492-USL, Lafayette, LA 70501 (Tel: 318-234-2835)

MARYLAND

Brookside Gardens, 1500 Glenallan Avenue, Wheaton, MD 20902 (Tel: 301-949-8230)

MASSACHUSETTS

Arnold Arboretum, The Arborway, Jamaica Plain, MA 02130 (Tel: 617-524-1717)

Garden in the Woods, New England Wildflower Society, Hemenway Road, Framingham, MA 01701 (Tel: 617-877-6574)

NEW JERSEY

Skylands Garden of Ringwood State Park, Box 1304, Ringwood, NJ 07456 (Tel: 201-962-7031)

Willowwood Arboretum of Rutgers Arboretum, Gladstone, NJ 07934 (Tel: 201-234-1246)

NEW YORK

Bayard Cutting Arboretum, Box 66, Oakdale, NY 11769 (Tel: 516-581-1002)

Brooklyn Botanic Garden, 1000 Washington Avenue, Brooklyn, NY 11225 (Tel: 212-622-4433)

Cornell Plantations, 100 Judd Falls Road, Ithaca, NY 14850 (Tel: 607-256-3020)

New York Botanical Garden, Bronx Park, Bronx, NY 10458

Old Westbury Gardens, Box 430, Old Westbury Road, Old Westbury, NY 11568 (Tel: 516-333-0048)

Planting Fields Arboretum, Planting Fields Road, Box 58, Oyster Bay, NY 11771 (Tel: 516-922-9206)

Queens Botanical Garden Society Inc., 43-50 Main Street, Flushing, NY 11355 (Tel: 212-886-3800)

NORTH CAROLINA

Clarendon Gardens, Linden Road, Pinecrest, NC 28374
North Carolina State University Botanical Garden, Raleigh
Orton Plantation Gardens, Wilmington, NC 28401 (Tel: 919–763–8587)
Reynolda Gardens, Wake Forest University, Box 7325 Reynolda Station, Winston-Salem, NC 27109 (Tel: 919–684–9711)
University Botanical Gardens of Asheville Inc., University of North Carolina, Asheville, NC 28804 (Tel: 704–254–7415)

OHIO

Dawes Arboretum, Route 5, Box 270, Newark, OH 43055 (Tel: 614–345–2355)
Mt Airy Forest and Arboretum, 5083 Colerain Avenue, Cincinnati, OH 45223 (Tel: 513–541–8176)
Secrest Arboretum, Ohio Agricultural Research and Development Center, Wooster, OH 44691 (Tel: 216–264–1021)
The Holden Arboretum, 9500 Sperry Road, Mentor, OH 44060 (Tel: 216–946–4400)

OKLAHOMA

Will Rogers Park, 3500 NW 36th Street, Oklahoma City, OK 73112 (Tel: 405–943–3977)

OREGON

Portland International Rose Test Garden, Washington Park, 400 SW Kingston Avenue, Portland, OR 97201 (Tel: 503–227–1911)
The American Rhododendron Society, Crystal Springs Rhododendron Garden, SE 28th near Woodstock Blvd., Portland, OR 97202

PENNSYLVANIA

Arthur Hoyt Scott Horticultural Foundation, Swarthmore College, Swarthmore, PA 19061 (Tel: 215–447–7025)
Hershey Rose Gardens and Arboretum, Hershey, PA 17033 (Tel: 717–534–3531)
Longwood Gardens, Kennett Square, PA 19348 (Tel: 215–388–6741)
Swiss Pines, Box 127, Charlestown Road, Malvern, PA 19355
Taylor Memorial Arboretum, 10 Ridley Drive, Garden City, Wallingford, PA 19086

The John J. Tyler Arboretum, 515 Painter Road, P.O. Box 216, Lima, PA 19060 (Tel: 215–566–5431)

The Morris Arboretum, University of Pennsylvania, 9414 Meadowbank Avenue, Philadelphia, PA 19118 (Tel: 215–243–500)

SOUTH CAROLINA

Brookgreen Gardens, Murrels Inlet, SC 29576 (Tel: 803–237–4657)

Cypress Gardens, Charleston, SC 29404 (Tel: 803–534–6376)

Magnolia Garden, Charleston, SC 29407 (Tel: 803–766–3642)

Middleton Place, Charleston Place, Charleston, SC 29407 (Tel: 803–556–6020)

TENNESSEE

Memphis Botanic Garden, Audubon Park, 750 Cherry Road, Memphis, TN 38117 (Tel: 901–685–1566)

Tennessee Botanical Gardens and Fine Arts Center, Cheekwood Cheek Road, Nashville, TN 37205 (Tel: 615–356–3306)

University of Tennessee Arboretum, 901 Kerr Hollow Road, Oak Ridge, TN 37830 (Tel: 615–683–8721)

VIRGINIA

Norfolk Botanical Gardens, Airport Road, Norfolk, VA 23518 (Tel: 804–855–0194)

WASHINGTON

Hiram Chittenden Locks, U.S. Army Corps of Engineers, Seattle District Office, 1519 Alaskan Way South, Seattle, WA 90134

University of Washington Arboretum, Seattle, WA 98195 (Tel: 206–543–8800)

Rhododendron Species Foundation, Federal Way, Box 3798, WA 98003 (Tel: 206–927–6960)

WEST VIRGINIA

West Virginia University Arboretum, Department of Biology, West Virginia University, Morgantown, WV 26506 (Tel: 304–293–4794)

Appendix 8
Nurseries Supplying Rhododendron Species, Varieties and Cultivars

This following list is in no way comprehensive.

British Isles

Braevallich Nursery (wholesale only), by Dalmally, Argyll, Scotland PA33 1BU
Exbury Estate, Exbury, Southampton, Hampshire
Glendoick Gardens Limited, Perth, Scotland PH2 7NS
Hillier and Sons, Winchester, Hampshire
Hydon Nurseries Limited, Clock Barn Lane, Hydon Heath, Godalming, Surrey
Miss King & Paton, Barnhourie, by Dalbeattie, Scotland DG5 4PU
Millais Nurseries, Crosswater Farm, Churt, Farnham, Surrey
Morley Nurseries (wholesale), Morley, Wymondham, Norfolk
Notcutts Nurseries Limited, Woodbridge, Suffolk
G. Reuthe Limited, Roxhill Nurseries, Jackass Lane, Keston, Kent
Slocock Nurseries, Barrs Lane, Knaphill, Woking, Surrey
F. Street, Heathermead Nursery, Fenns Lane, West End, Woking, Surrey
Waterers Nurseries, Bagshot, Surrey (including Dobbies and Company, Melville Nurseries, Lasswade, Midlothian)

Canada

Woodland Nurseries, 2151 Camilla Road, Mississauga, Ontario L5A 2K1

Denmark

Tue Jorgensen, Ryvej 10, DK 2830, Virrn, Denmark

New Zealand

Blue Mountain Nurseries, Bushy Hill Street, Tapanui, Otago
Mr B. W. Campbell, 20A Waireka Street, Ravensbourne, Dunedin
Kentons Nurseries, 311 Wakari Road, Dunedin
Opoho Nurseries, Mowat Street, Dunedin

United States of America

Bovees Nursery, 1737 S.W. Coronado, Portland, Oregon 97219
Farwell's Rhododendron and Azalea Nursery, 13040 Skyline Boulevard, Woodside, California 94062
Garden Valley Nursery, 12960 N.E. 181st, Bothell, Washington 98011
Gordner's Rhododendron Nursery Inc., 27402 –114th S.E., Kent, Washington 98031
Greer's Gardens, 1280 Goodpasture Island Road, Eugene, Oregon 97401
Hall Rhododendrons, 1280 Quince Drive, Junction City, Oregon 97488
Hart's Nursery Inc., 1578 Best Road, Mt. Vernon, Washington
Horsley Rhododendron Nursery, 7441 Tracyton Boulevard, N.W., Bremerton, Washington 98310 (does not ship)
Larson's Rhododendrons and Azaleas, 3656 Bridgeport Way, Tacoma, Washington 98466
Rhododendron Species Foundation, P.O. Box 3798, Federal Way, WA 98003
Van Veen's Nursery, 4205 S.E. Franklin, Portland, Oregon 97206
Whitney Gardens, P.O. Box F, Brinnon, Washington 98320

West Germany

Dietrich G. Hobbie, Rhododendron–Kulturen, Linswege, 2910 Westerstede 1

Appendix 9
Organisations Providing Guide Books or Other Literature

Historic Irish Tourist Houses and Gardens Association, 3a Castle Street, Dalkey, County Dublin, Republic of Ireland (Tel: 0001–801618)

National Gardens Scheme, 57 Lower Belgrave Street, London SW1W 0LR (Tel: 01–730–0359)

National Trust, 42 Queen Anne's Gate, London SW1H 9AS (Tel: 01–222–9251)

National Trust for Scotland, 5 Charlotte Square, Edinburgh EH2 4DU (Tel: 031–226–5922; 041–332–7277)

Royal Botanic Garden, Inverleith Row, Edinburgh EH3 5LR (Tel: 031–552–7171)

Royal Botanic Gardens, Kew, Kew Road, London (Tel: 01–940–1171)

Royal Horticultural Society, Vincent Square, London SW1 2PE (Tel: 01–834–4333)

Scotland Garden Scheme, The General Organiser, 26 Castle Terrace, Edinburgh EH1 2EL (Tel: 031–229–1870)

Glossary of Botanical Terms

Many of the following terms have been used in this book while others have been included to enable the reader to understand the meaning of certain other terminology to be found in literature on the genus. Complicated descriptions have been simplified where possible.

Actinomorphic   Radially symmetrical; when a flower is bisected at any point through the vertical plane the two halves will be mirror images.

Adpressed (appressed)   Lying flat or close together.

Acute   Sharply pointed.

Agglutinate   Glued together.

Annular   Ring-shaped.

Anther   Part of the stamen containing pollen grains.

Auricle (auriculate)   Ear-like appendage or projection often used to describe the shape of the base of a leaf.

Axillary   Growing out of the angle between the upper side of a leaf and the stem on which the leaf is borne.

Bullate   Blistered or puckered.

Calcifuge   Literally 'avoiding limestone'.

Campanulate   Bell-shaped (generally of flowers).

Calyx   Outermost part of flower, composed of the sepals.

Capsule   Dry dehiscent fruit, as found in the rhododendron.

Chlorophyll   Green colouring pigment of plants.

Chlorosis   Pale green or yellow colouration of foliage due to the death or masking of chlorophyll.

Chromosome(s)   Rod-like bodies found in the cell nucleus and visible only when the cell is dividing.

Ciliate   Fringed with hairs.

Clone   Vegetatively produced progeny of a single plant.

Contiguous   Touching at the edges.

Cordate   Heart-shaped (generally of leaves).

Coriaceous   Leathery.

Corolla   Part of flower, within the calyx, consisting of the petals.

Cotyledon(s)   Seed leaves which are already present in the seed prior to germination.

Cultivar   Literally a cultivated variety.

Deciduous   Losing leaves at a certain season, e.g. autumn.

Eglandular   Without glands.

Elepidote   Without scales.

Endemic   Confined to a given area.

Epigeal   Where the seed leaves appear above ground level during germination.

Epiphyte   A plant growing on another but deriving no nourishment from it.

Fertile   Bearing seeds which are capable of germinating.

Fertilisation   Union of two gametes to produce a zygote. In plants, the gametes are carried in the pollen grain and the ovule and unite to produce a seed.

Floccose   Bearing tufts of soft woolly hair.

Gene   Units of inheritance found on the chromosome which govern the development and structure of the plant.

Genus   A group of related species or subgenera.

Glabresecent   Becoming glabrous.

Glabrous   Without hairs.

Gland   Small vesicle, secreting an oil or resin, found on the surface or protruding from any part of the plant; often associated with hairs.

Glandular   Possessing glands.

Glaucous   Bluish or possessing grey-blue bloom.

Grex   Name given to all seedlings resulting from a cross.

Hastate   Spear-shaped; usually applied to the leaf.

Hirsute   Hairy, clothed with long hairs.

Hybrid   Result of a cross between genetically dissimilar parents, e.g. two species, a species and a hybrid, two hybrids or even two genera.

Hybrid swarm   Group of plants, usually but not necessarily wild, in which each plant may differ from another as well as from the parent plants. The result of hybridisation between two species followed by crossing and backcrossing of subsequent generations. Identification can be very difficult as they will not key out exactly.

Indumentum   Woolly or hairy covering, found on the leaves of many rhododendrons. The colour and form can be useful for identification purposes.

Inflorescence   Simple or complex branch of the plant which bears a number of flowers.

Internode   Part of stem between two nodes.

Key Means of identifying species, and sometimes hybrids, using a series of contrasting characteristics.

Lamina Blade of a leaf or occasionally a petal.

Lanceolate Lance-shaped, where the length is approximately three times the breadth.

Lepidote Covered in small scales. A major division of the genus *Rhodendron* in which the foliage, and frequently the flowers, have this characteristic.

Ligulate Strap-shaped.

Linear Where the leaves are at least twelve times as long as broad.

Mucronate Possessing a short, sharp, narrow point.

Mycorrhiza Symbiotic relationship between plant root and fungus.

Nectar (nectary) Sugary fluid secreted by glands, usually found at the interior base of the corolla. Used to attract insects which help to pollinate the flowers.

Node (nodal) Point of attachment of the leaves to the stem.

Nomenclature The scientific naming of plants and animals.

Oblong Where the leaves are twice as long as they are broad, with the sides parallel for some distance.

Obovate Where the length is greater than the breadth, widest point towards apex.

Orbicular Where the leaves are approximately as long as they are broad.

Ovary Body which contains the ovules.

Ovate Applied to foliage where the length is just greater than the breadth, the broadest section being nearer the base.

Ovule Structure, which, when fertilised, develops ino the seed.

Papilla Small projection.

Pedicel Stalk of a single flower in an inflorescence.

Peduncle Stalk of an inflorescence or a solitary flower.

Perianth Outer part of flower, enclosing stamens and carpels, usually consisting of calyx and corolla.

Petiole Leaf-stalk.

Pilose With long, soft hairs.

Plastered indumentum Having a smooth finish.

Pollen Minute usually single-celled structures (but 4-celled in the rhododendron) containing male gametes.

Pollination Transfer of pollen from anther to stigma.

Prostrate Creeping, or growing more or less flat to the ground.

Pubescent Soft downy hair.

Puberulent, puberulous Partially covered with soft downy hair.

166

Raceme   Inflorescence where the flowers open from the base upwards.

Reticulate   Network of veins.

Revolute   Rolled downwards.

Rugose   Wrinkled.

Rugulose   Slightly wrinkled or rough.

Scabrid   Rough to the touch.

Scales   Small round dots found on the leaves, stem and flowers of the lepidote division of *Rhododendron*.

Serrate, serrulate   With very small teeth like a saw.

Sessile   Without a stalk; usually, in *Rhododendron,* with reference to leaves.

Setose   Covered with bristles.

Species   A group of closely related, interbreeding individuals showing consistent differences from allied groups.

Stamen   Male reproductive organ in a flower, composed of anther and filament.

Sterile   Unable to reproduce sexually.

Stigma   Part of the female reproductive unit which receives the pollen.

Stipitate   Having a short stalk.

Stoma(ta)   Pore in the epidermis of plants, particularly abundant on the underside of the leaves, which permits the exchange of gases, e.g. oxygen, carbon dioxide and water vapour.

Strigose   Clothed with stiff adpressed hairs.

Style   Extension of the carpel which ends in the stigma.

Taxon   A category, of any rank, in botanical or zoological classification.

Taxonomist   Person who studies the classification of plants (or animals).

Terminal bud   Last bud on a growing shoot.

Tomentum   Dense woolly covering of hairs.

Undulate   Wavy.

Viscid   Sticky.

Zygomorphic   Bilaterally symmetrical.

Bibliography

General

Cox, E. H. M., *Rhododendrons for Amateurs*, Country Life Ltd, 1924.

Cox, E. H. M. and Cox, P. A., *Modern Rhododendrons*, Nelson, 1955.

Cox, Peter, *Wisley Handbook No. 2. Rhododendrons*, Royal Horticultural Society, London, 1972.

Cox, Peter, *Dwarf Rhododendrons*, Batsford, London, 1973.

Cox, Peter, *The Larger Species of Rhododendron*, Batsford, London, 1979.

Fairweather, Christopher, *Rhododendrons and Azaleas for Your Garden*, Floraprint Ltd, 1979.

Kingdon-Ward, Frank, *Rhododendrons*, Latimer House Ltd, 1949.

Leach, D. F., *Rhododendrons of the World*, George Allan and Unwin, London, 1962.

Rhododendron Year Book 1946→ [Rhododendron and Camellia Yearbook; Rhododendrons with Magnolias and Camellias], Royal Horticultural Society, London.

Street, Frederick, *Hardy Rhododendrons*, Collins, Glasgow, 1954.

Historical

These publications are normally only available through botanical gardens and similar institutes. Journals are also published by the specialist rhododendron societies (see Appendix 6).

Hooker, J. D., *Rhododendrons of Sikkim Himalayas*, Reeve, 1851.

Journal of the Royal Horticultural Society 1875–1975 [*The Garden* 1975→].

Millais, J. G., *Rhododendrons and Their Various Hybrids*, Longmans, Green and Company, 1917 and 1924.

Identification and Nomenclature

Bean, W. J., *Trees and Shrubs Hardy in the British Isles*, John Murray, London, 1976.

Cowan, J. M., *The Rhododendron Leaf*, Oliver and Boyd, Edinburgh, 1950.

Cullen, J., 'Revision of *Rhododendron*. I Subgenus *Rhododendron* section Rhododendron and Pogonanthum'. *Notes from the Royal Botanic Gardens Edinburgh*, 1980, v. 39, 1–207.

Cullen, J. and Chamberlain, D. F. 'A preliminary synopsis of the genus *Rhododendron*'. *Notes from the Royal Botanic Gardens Edinburgh*, 1980, v. 36, 105–126.

Cullen, J. and Chamberlain, D. F., 'A preliminary synopsis of the genus *Rhododendron* II'. *Notes from the Royal Botanic Gardens Edinburgh*, 1979, v. 37, 327–338.

Curtis's Botanical Magazine 1790, Royal Horticultural Society, London.

International Rhododendron Register (and Supplements), Royal Horticultural Society, London.

Journal of the Royal Horticultural Society 1875–1975 [*The Garden* 1975 →].

Philipson, M. N. and Philipson, W. R. 'A revision of *Rhododendron* section Lapponica'. *Notes from the Royal Botanic Gardens Edinburgh*, 1975, v. 34, 1–72.

Rhododendron Handbook 1947, Royal Horticultural Society, London.

Rhododendron Handbook 1952, Royal Horticultural Society, London.

Rhododendron Handbook 1964. Part Two. Rhododendron Hybrids, Royal Horticultural Society, London.

Rhododendron Handbook 1980. Rhododendron Species in Cultivation, Royal Horticultural Society, London.

Rhododendron Yearbook 1946 → [*Rhododendron and Camellia Yearbook; Rhododendrons with Magnolias and Camellias*], Royal Horticultural Society, London.

Stevenson, J. B. (Editor), *The Species of Rhododendron*, Royal Horticultural Society, 1930.

Yearbook of the Rhododendron Association 1938, Royal Horticultural Society, London.

Collectors and Collecting

Cowan, J. M. and Royal Horticultural Society, *George Forrest — Journeys and Plant Introductions,* Oxford University Press, 1952.

Kingdon-Ward, Frank, *Plant Hunting on the Edge of the World,* Victor Gollancz, 1930.

Kingdon-Ward, Frank, *Plant Hunting in the Wild,* Figurehead, 1931.

Kingdon-Ward, Frank, *A Plant Hunter in Tibet,* Jonathan Cape, London, 1937.

Kingdon-Ward, Frank, *Modern Explorations,* Jonathan Cape, London, 1945.

Kingdon-Ward, Frank, *Burma's Icy Mountains,* Jonathan Cape, London, 1949.

Kingdon-Ward, Frank, *Plant Hunting in Manipur,* Jonathan Cape, London, 1952.

Kingdon-Ward, Frank, *Return to the Irrawaddy,* Andrew Melrose, London, 1956.

Kingdon-Ward, Frank, *Pilgrimage for Plants,* Harrap, 1960.

Kraxberger, Meldon (Editor), *American Rhododendron Hybrids,* The American Rhododendron Society, 1980.

Luteyn, James L. and O'Brien, Mary E. (Editors), *Contributions Toward a Classification of Rhododendrons. Proceedings of the International Rhododendron Conference, New York Botanic Garden, 1980.*

Index of Colour Plates

General Index

Numbers in *italic* refer to black and white illustrations.